It Don't Make Sense Not to Trust God
By Dr. Toni Boulware Stackhouse

All rights reserved. No part of this publication may be reproduced, stored in a retrieval system, or transmitted in any way, by any means – electronic, mechanical, digital, photocopy, recording, or otherwise – without permission of the author, except as provided by the United States of America copyright law.

Copyright © August, 2019 by Dr. Toni Boulware Stackhouse
Published by Pecan Tree Publishing

Unless otherwise noted, all Scripture quotations are from the King James Version of the Bible.

Scripture quotations marked AMP are from THE AMPLIFIED BIBLE, Old Testament copyright © 1965, 1987 by the Zondervan Corporation. The Amplified New Testament copyright © 1958, 1987 by The Lockman Foundation. Used by permission.

Scripture quotations marked NIV are from the HOLY BIBLE, NEW INTERNATIONAL VERSION. Copyright © 1973, 1978, 1984 by International Bible Society. Used by permission of Zondervan Publishing House. All rights reserved.

978-1-7358295-8-6 Paperback
979-8-9855014-0-7 E-book
Library of Congress Catalog Number: 2021904411

Cover design by: Glenda Antonio
Interior and E-book design by: Charlyn Samson
Cover photo and author photo by: Aisha Butler Photography

Pecan Tree Publishing
www.pecantreebooks.com

New Voices | New Styles | New Vision –
Creating a New Legacy of Dynamic Authors and Titles
Hollywood, FL

It Don't Make Sense Not to Trust God

Dr. Toni Boulware Stackhouse

PRAISE FOR IT DON'T MAKE SENSE NOT TO TRUST GOD

Terrific book! Very proud of your testimony. I love what God is doing in both your lives. You are a mighty woman of God and you have been faithful. He has made you're a ruler! God bless you!—Benjamin

Dr. Toni thanks for sharing your faith story with all of us. You are a mighty woman of God. God blessed you both with each other Your faith is a reminder of why we need to trust God. Your response to the doctors reminds me of when my baby was four months old, and she was diagnosed with achondroplasia and doctors said most kids don't live to be a year old. I said, "Doc, thanks for your diagnosis but I serve a God in heaven. You are a professional in your field. But my faith will take care of her." She is four years old as I write these words and outside playing. With faith all things are possible.—Supermumze

Your book is truly internally impacting. I'm at the doctor's office and while waiting, reading your book, and twice I had to put it down because I was going to start crying. Not only because of the tumultuous experience, but also for truth of God's faithfulness. God is marvelous!!—Cousin Sloane

The book is phenomenal, spiritually moving, thought provoking, and comforting to those who are experiencing similar challenges. Thank you, Toni. God is blessing us through you.—Kevin Johnson

The book is awesome, life changing, pushing one to greatness, purpose driven. It will make you submit to God's will for life and surrender your plans to the Almighty God. Thank you so much Dr. Toni. I love you and Sam.—Tivoli Artis

CONTENTS

Dedication ix
Acknowledgments xi
Introduction xv

Chapter 1: It Don't Make Sense! 1
Chapter 2: Wisdom and Knowledge 9
Chapter 3: When God Interrupts 13
Chapter 4: Making Sense of Faith 37
Chapter 5: I Have Found Grace to be Amazing! 47
Chapter 6: New Things Spring Up 51
Chapter 7: Perfect Conditions 63
Chapter 8: Mourning the Loss of My Husband 67
Chapter 9: The Weight of the Wait 81
Chapter 10: Finality 89

About the Author 93

DEDICATION

I DEDICATE THIS BOOK TO my husband Samuel A. Stackhouse III whom I love dearly and have had the pleasure of having my faith infused to another dimension because of the journey that him and I have shared for the last four plus years. Sam you are my miracle man full of joy and enthusiasm for life even in this. I thank God for your determination and will to live life against all the odds that were stacked against you. You have been determined to push beyond the limitations in search of new life and God has exceeded all expectations. You have given so much love and laughter through this storm and that has been encouraging! Your desire to love and encourage others despite your own challenges has been nothing short of amazing. Although unexpected this journey has created in us a great union that makes for a great foundation in marriage. I can only imagine where life will lead us from here. I'm so excited about our future together because I know that it is filled with great anticipation. The enemy came for us, and we persevered by the grace of God. I'm so excited to do life with you on God's terms. After this, it don't make sense not to trust God!

ACKNOWLEDGMENTS

I WOULD LIKE TO THANK God who is amazing; and without Him there is nothing to testify about. He has been my grace; helping me to maintain balance in an unsteady place and for THIS I give Him praise!

Next, I would like to thank my family, who have been without question, a very sure source of support. They have stood with Sam and I since August 23, 2017 and continue standing with us through this arduous journey.

My parents are true gems, loving and caring for Sam as their very own son. They've been there for medical appointments and transportation to and from Richmond, Virginia for rehabilitation. They are the best for providing us this kind of support in their retirement. I am most grateful!

My daughter and son-son who rock, ensuring that I am always well cared for. My daughter who ensured that I was never alone at the hospital and when things got tough, she reached out to other family members for additional support.

My Sistah! - Dr. Paula Boulware Brown and brother-in-love Pastor J walked in faith with us, encouraging us in meaningful ways.

My brother and sister from another mother, Dr. Derren and Chalon; Sam's mother Minister Stephanie Walters, Uncle Richard, Aunt Theresa, and Uncle George for your support. You are appreciated!

All the other family and friends for your prayers and support.

We want to thank Bishop Ronald G. and Pastor Angela King and Apostle Keith and Prophetess Carnetta McDuffie and ministry for your prayers and support. We especially want to thank our Spiritual Father Archbishop Ralph L Dennis and Lady Deborah Dennis and family for their prayers and support!

Sam and I have had a host of family and friends praying us through this journey and we could not have made it without you all. I pray God's multiplied blessings on your life for blessing us!!!

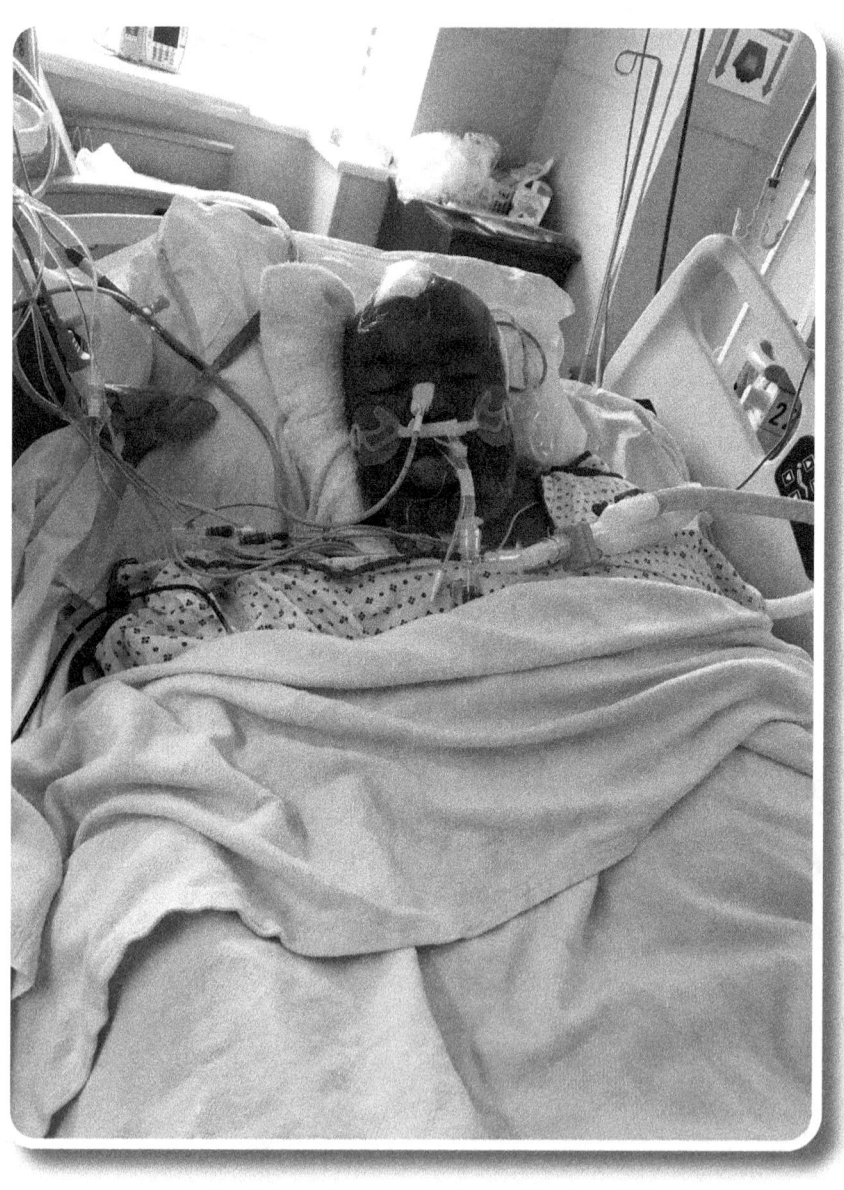

INTRODUCTION

ONE DAY WHEN I was struggling to mentally and emotionally make sense of all of this that we were experiencing, I vacillated between why this tragedy transpired in our life and how it would end. I was pondering if I could do what God was calling me to do amid all that was occurring in my life. I was questioning God about how He was going to do what He promised. I was wondering if we would experience the move of God that we so desperately desired. And since it had not happened yet, would God even perform this miracle for us.

Then it happened, it came to me in a small still voice just as clear as day but emphatically, "it don't make sense not to trust God!" I came to myself and realized that this was indeed the case. How could I not trust a God who has been faithful to me all my life? During that moment I reminisced about all the things that God had already performed in my life. The fact that I am even alive is a miracle. A month after giving birth to my daughter by Cesarean section at the age of 17, doctors told my parents I wouldn't live through the night. Blood clots had consumed space in my lungs. I saw God's miraculous hand in the way He divinely provided a way out of no way for Sam and me to take possession of the home that we built just 45 days prior to him experiencing the massive stroke I talk about in this book. Surely God has proven Himself to be a very present help as David penned in Psalms 46.

Sometimes we get caught up in the minutia of things trying to figure out just how God is going to do what He has promised to do. And we need to understand that knowing the entire plan and result is not our concern. Our only responsibility in the matter is to trust God. Trusting God requires us to move forward - with our part - in what He is requiring from us. That is faith in action! The Word of God in James 2:14, declares that faith without works is dead. We are required of God to align our actions with what we ask Him to do for us. For example, if we ask God for a job, that will require us to prepare a resume, apply for desired positions and participate in interviews. Otherwise, how can we expect to obtain a job without putting faith into action, which informs God of our anticipation. Knowing that God has His part under control even when it seems like nothing is happening or moving in the direction that we want it to. God is faithful and His track record precedes Him. He needs no help from us other than the faith and obedience required to experience a performance from an Almighty God.

My quandary initially was whether to move forward in ministry or wait until my understanding of full manifestation of promise occurred. Then I realized my understanding of full manifestation is faulty at best. God is looking for obedience, despite how it looks and regardless of what we are facing. We have to choose to have the kind of faith in God that supersedes what we are feeling. Feelings change and we need to ensure that we are in control of our emotions lest we allow ourselves to miss God and the opportunity to have Him move in our lives.

This book is about manifesting purpose and faith in the Earth regardless of the challenges that may exist. We are all called to manifest the things that God has placed inside of us before we were placed in the womb. You will read something in this book that will encourage you to be who God created you to be without hesitation and resistance!

Because it don't make sense not to trust God!

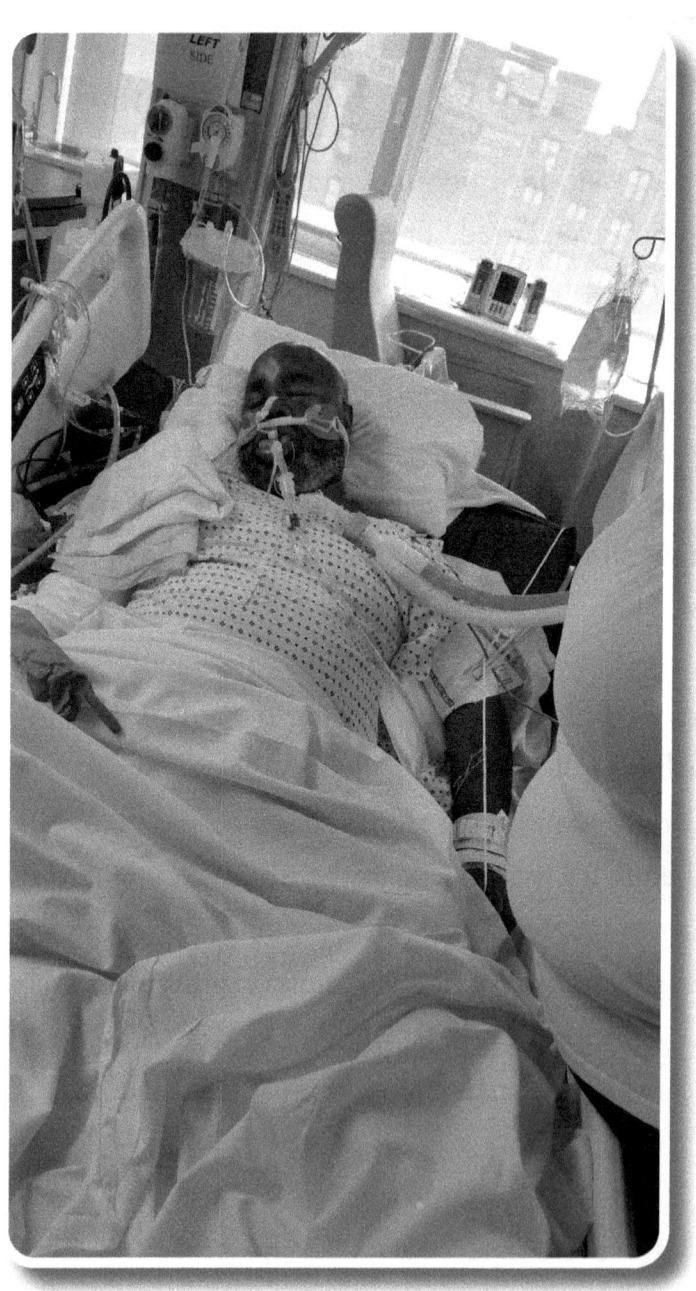

CHAPTER ONE

It Don't Make Sense!

GOD ESTABLISHED HIS FAITHFULNESS to the Earth long before we were placed into existence. This display of love in action occurred when He spoke things into existence during creation and those things are still manifesting in the Earth today. In Genesis 1, it says that the Earth was without form and was void. God spoke light into darkness and there was light. He then separated the light and darkness into day and night. We live with the light that He spoke and do so without thought for it. However, we depend on that light occurring day after day. Without the light there would be chaos across the land. But because He spoke it, we have the assurance that it will occur without incident.

It was also no coincidence that during the creation story God created us in His image and likeness, meaning we resemble Him so spiritually we should be like Him. We should be able to speak things into existence and it manifest. Our life journey should resemble Him through the Holy Spirit who is our helper in the Earth. The Holy Spirit helps us to manifest God in the Earth realm. The plan of God is enacted through His people. We are His hands and feet. We yield to His desire when we surrender and submit to Him.

Everything that God has set into motion occurs without hesitation or delay. Every day the sun rises and every evening it sets regardless of the weather conditions. Even when it was a cloudy or a rainy day the sun still rose and set. When I was younger, I believed that when the weather was rainy or cloudy that the sun was not active. One day it was raining, and I was listening to the weather forecast and the weatherman gave the times that the sun would rise and set, and I was amazed. I had no idea prior to that moment that when the weather was adverse that the sun was still going to rise and set. Of course, it was going to rise and set because God created it to do so regardless of the conditions. And so, when God created us to be in the Earth realm it was not based on conditions but despite them. However, we sometimes struggle with this and because we do something is lacking in the Earth and it is waiting for us to manifest!

Creation is moaning and groaning for the children of God to manifest Him fully! The Earth needs us to be who God created us to be point blank without hesitation and resistance. God created us to be a solution to a problem in the Earth and that is why the Earth is groaning for the solution to the problems that exist. People need the salvation of God, healing, and deliverance from the wickedness of the enemy. For some of us, this is not our focus because we live with a certain level of freedom in God. We must remember when we were desperate for God, He used someone – His Son - to rescue us from whatever ailed us.

Why are we not manifesting and becoming who God designed us to be? Why do we allow our external conditions to affect us in a way that causes us to be inactive to the will of God for our lives? With God, we always win. Knowing this we sometimes struggle in just becoming or being who God created us to be and operating in the gifts that God has placed inside of us and being in His will for our lives. Is this a trust issue when we say we have faith in God and that He is faithful? Then why do our actions rarely line up with this declaration? We must understand that faith is not only declarations, but it is accompanied with acts of obedience that directly line up with what we believe. Faith is not about having God meet our self-motivated desires. Our faith should trust in the plan that God has for our lives. Most times we want God's plans on our agenda and that affects our abilities to see the manifestations of what we believe for. The Bible says seek first the Kingdom of God then and only then will He add all those other things to us. We want things first then we will consider what God desires from us. God had plans for our lives prior to our birth and we have been so busy presenting Him with our agendas that we missed the mark on what is at stake when we fail to manifest who we are to be in the Earth. Yes, a problem remains unresolved. There are some people waiting in need of salvation, healing, and deliverance and diverse forms of challenges, valleys, laments and suffering until we decide to operate in purpose. The process of becoming is different for each of us, yet it is through our situations and circumstances that God activates the gifts inside of us for His purpose for our lives. Otherwise, they lie dormant within us until we seek God's guidance for our purpose.

How is creation still trusting God after all these years despite our daily failure to manifest our purpose and calling? Because God is sovereign, and His will shall always come to pass. Imagine not becoming who God has created you to be. We make all kinds of excuses about why we can't be who God has created us to be. In doing so, we also fail to think about the condition of those people who we are supposed to have an impact on. Our disobedience to the mandate of God for us affects those we have been divinely assigned to. How would you feel to discover the person who God selected to use to answer your prayer request was somewhere making excuses and being disobedient? Frustrated? Angry? Disappointed? The people whom you are supposed to have an impact on are waiting for you to decide that now is the time to manifest. We are God's hands and feet in the Earth. He uses His children to accomplish His desires.

What if the sun made excuses about why it could not rise or set? What chaos would that create in the Earth? What if the moon decided not to shine at night? What darkness would befall the Earth? God saved the Earth from darkness and provided light. If the sun did not rise, there would be darkness across the Earth in the same way that we see darkness in the lives of people because we failed to operate in the manner in which God created us to do so.

One thing we never have to worry about is whether there is going to be daylight even if the sun doesn't shine it rises. That speaks to the faithfulness of God and His provision for us. He has given us everything we need in the Earth to be successful. We use continuous excuses not to do God's will, which attempted to make God look like He is not faithful in the lives of those individuals counting on us to manifest. This is far from being true. God has a plan of salvation for all of us and that is not just about securing you a place in heaven. This speaks to His plan to save you from the plans of the enemy here on Earth even when the enemy is ourselves. He wants to save us from ourselves most times. It is our way of thinking that causes us to delay in what He is calling us to do.

In the same manner that God spoke to the sun and the moon and gave them direction on what to do, He has also spoken to us in conversation about who we are to become. In Jeremiah it says before I formed you, I knew you. In Him saying that he knew us that translates to I know what I purposed you to be and then I placed you in your mother's womb for you to enter the Earth and become just that. If this is the truth, when God speaks to us to do some things, then why do we make all kinds of excuses about why we cannot fulfill the assignment? Surely if the sun can rise and set in adverse conditions, this is an indication to you and me that things will not always be perfect but that does not preclude you from being who God created you to be. In fact, we need to use those challenges as motivation to be determined to become who He created us to be. Usually when we pushed forward, we found that those conditions eventually subsided. And had we not moved we would have missed an opportunity to not only become who God created us to be but to see Him deliver victory to us. We always win. Obedience to God's plan for our lives secures that victory for sure!

The adversary's desire is to prevent us from becoming who God has created us to be. He will try to place obstacles in our way to preclude God's desires for our lives. We should use that as our motivation to keep moving forward regardless of what the adversary may try to throw our way because we are not ignorant to his devises. His schemes have already been revealed to us. His desire is to steal, kill or destroy. Sometimes we have allowed him to do that without even a fight. It is like we did not value the treasure that God has placed inside of us. We have to begin to see the value of God creating us and His intent. And once we discover this purpose, we should seek diligently after that because that is where we find the greatest victories of life. It is shameful people have lived and died never having scratched the surface of God's purpose for their lives. This world is full of people wandering aimlessly not having any idea of who or how to seek purpose in their lives. For some of us our purpose is helping to point people in God's direction in search of His intent for creating them. Heaven forbid we miss this opportunity to assist those in becoming.

The Earth is groaning for you to be who God created you to become and someone is waiting on you!!!!

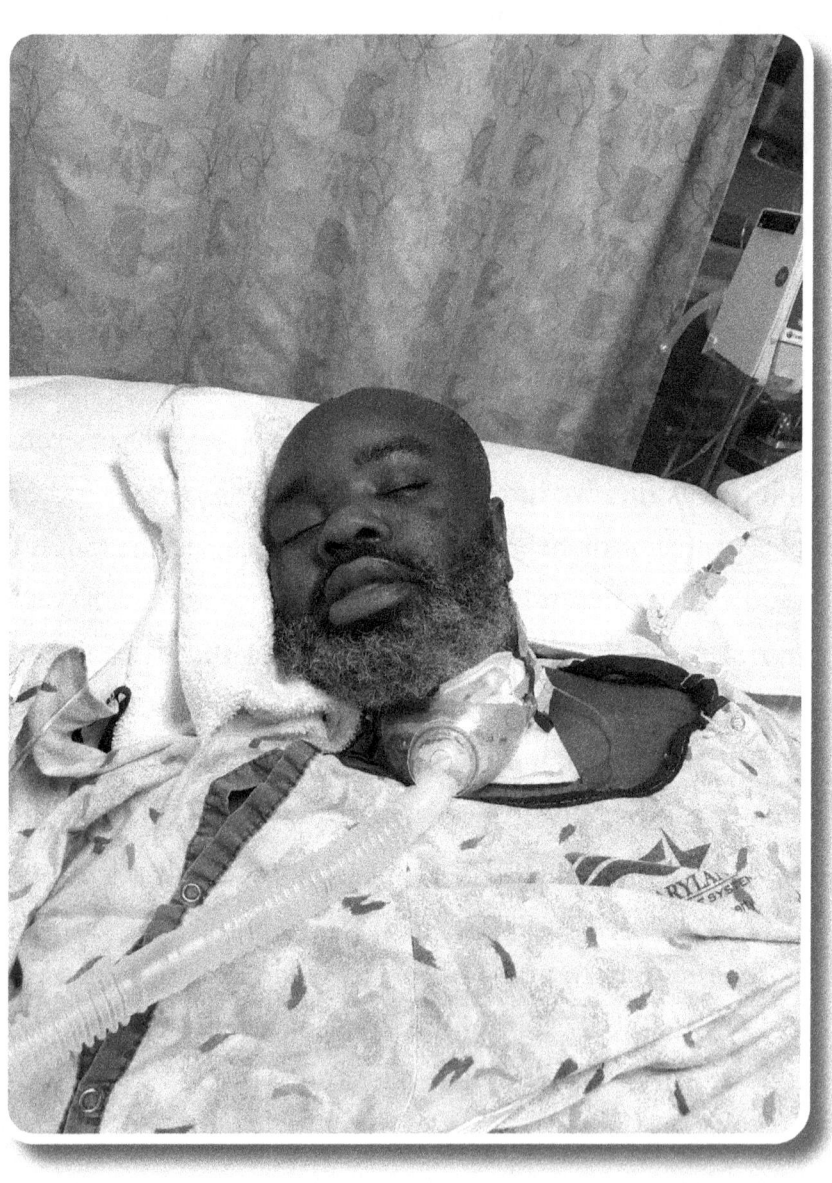

CHAPTER 2

Wisdom and Knowledge

WHATEVER PROFESSION WE FIND ourselves in, whether it is marketplace or ministry inside the church, it is the grace that is given from God for us to operate. When we submit the very gifts and talents that He has given to us back to Him, it is He who multiplies and blesses what we put our hands to. It is foolish for us to believe that outside of Him we have all the answers and know what the right moves are in all situations because this is not the case. Seeking God in all things, not just difficult things, is crucial. In those times when we are desperate, we are sure to find Him along with what we need. Sometimes what we needed from God was different from what we sought; however, when we trusted Him, we realized that they were the same. God knew what we need and when we needed it. Once God had released that to us, we found contentment in that. We didn't need prior understanding before God met the need. Trusting and seeking

God in the hard places can be challenging but remaining focused on the goal will help us to remain on the path that He is leading us on. When we did not have all the answers to our questions in challenging times that caused us to have anxiety and allowed fear to step in. And in the panic of not knowing, we stressed instead of relying on an all-knowing God who will not fail His children. By trusting in Him we find peace even in challenging times. His peace gives us assurance that He is present in our lives. This gives us assurance that this too will work out for my good. There is nothing like the peace of God and knowing that He has us in the palm of His hands. There is nothing that is a surprise to Him, and nothing can catch Him off guard. God has all the answers and in Him we are able to find all that we need.

The Bible declares whoever lacks wisdom let him ask for it. We all lack wisdom if we are not seeking the wisdom that only comes from an all-knowing God. Nothing supersedes the knowledge and wisdom of God! The Bible declares that God is all-knowing which means He operates from a place of knowing how everything will unfold. When we make plans, we do so from a limited perspective. When God has plans for us, He does so without limitations. He sees the entire picture. That is why it is key for us to trust Him knowing that He has more knowledge and wisdom than we do. When we find ourselves in situations that we are unsure of it is in our best interest to seek Him and the wisdom and knowledge that He wants to bestow upon us. In James 1:5 we are encouraged to ask for wisdom when we lack it. This is our opportunity to seek God and His Word says that He will give to us generously. When we operate in this manner, we have peace beyond our understanding. We are led to move in the direct path that God is guiding us into for His Will for our lives.

As we yield our will over to Him and learn more about Him that trust increases, and our faith is exercised. As this occurs, we should be moving as we are led by God through His wisdom and knowledge, being assured that He has us where He wants us to be in that particular moment in time. Nothing just happens in our lives. God is intentional about what He does and what He allows. Purpose can be found through it all for a surrendered vessel earnestly seeking to know God more intimately which should be our goal. When we try to operate outside of God's wisdom, we find ourselves in situations and circumstances with no real direction for His intent. We have to understand that God has a plan based on His wisdom and knowledge and we are not able to discern that outside of Him. Nor should it be our desire to do so……

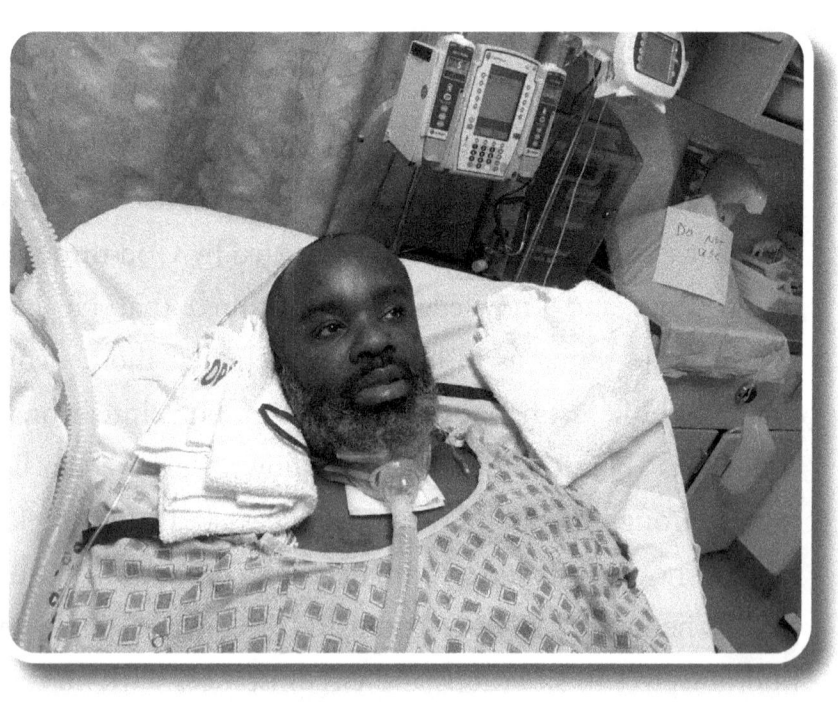

CHAPTER 3

When God Interrupts

WHEN GOD INTERRUPTS OUR regularly scheduled plans things can get interesting for sure. God often orchestrates interruptions for redirection. It takes spiritual discernment to ascertain what is transpiring and how to approach the interruption.

Wednesday, August 23rd, 2017, was a normal day for my husband and me. When I woke up, I realized that he was still at home which was not normal for him, because he usually left out for work before me. He said he was tired, was going to rest and go to work later. I proceeded to get dressed and before leaving for work he told me he would call when he left out for work. While I was at work, I noticed the time was late and I hadn't heard from him, so I called. When he answered the phone, he immediately laughed; he explained after he took his shower, he sat on the bed and had fallen back to sleep. We laughed and he said he would call once he left the house. He called around noon and advised he was going to work until 8 p.m. My husband was tired. The week prior we had just returned from Jamaica where we celebrated our second wedding anniversary. And the weekend after that we flew to Missouri to take our nephew to college. Our usual practice when returning home from being away was to take another day off to rest. This time we did not because of pressing tasks.

While at work Sam and I talked several times throughout the day which is usual for us, and all appeared normal. I remember leaving work early that day because I was tired after completing some tasks. When I arrived home, I started washing clothes from the suitcases and I took a nap. When I was in the laundry room washing clothes Sam sent me a text asking what was for dinner, but I did not realize that he had texted, so he called my phone at approximately 8:07 p.m. He asked if I received his text and I responded that I had not received it. He inquired about dinner, and I informed him that we were having leftovers. So, he informed me that he was on the way home and if anyone knows my husband that could be hours because he is either going to cross paths with someone he knows and talk to them for hours or he is going to meet someone new and talk to them for hours. So, I am like okay. When I talked to my husband, there was no sign of anything being wrong at all. It was a normal conversation.

Shortly after the phone conversation I heated up dinner and awaited his arrival. An hour later, I received a call from my sister-in-law. She told me the paramedics were with Sam and he had a medical emergency. I was shocked and surprised! I had spoken with Sam moments prior, and he sounded fine. Now what is going on? I asked her where he was and where were they taking him. Later I learned that the paramedics called the last person that Sam had called using the redial feature. His brother was the last person he had spoken to prior to becoming ill. I contacted my daughter, who lives around the corner from me, to come to pick me up. When we walked out my front door, the police were pulling Sam's car from the neighbor's lawn where Sam had driven while he was having the stroke. When the officer saw me coming out of the house he asked if I had been in the house for a while and I responded yes. He said he had been ringing the bell; but I did not hear anything. All this had happened in front of my house! Amazingly Sam made it home and rolled onto the neighbor's lawn. That neighbor happened to come out that night for a walk, as opposed to her normal Tuesday and Thursday walk. She shared she felt led by the Holy Spirit to go for a walk on Wednesday evening. So, she walked twice around the block and did not see Sam's car there and was compelled to take an additional walk around the block; the third time around she saw his car on the lawn and noticed him just sitting in the car. She decided to approach the car because she felt like something was wrong. She opened the passenger door. Her eyes and Sam's locked. He struggled to communicate but was trying with his eyes to indicate that something was wrong. She immediately called 911 and stayed with him until they arrived. Once the medical team arrived, they assessed him and immediately placed him in the ambulance to take him to the nearest hospital.

My head was spinning as my daughter and I followed the police officer to the emergency room where Sam was lying in the bed in major distress and unable to speak, although he was conscious. He was unable to move his right side. The medical staff conducted a series of assessments and discovered he might have been experiencing a Transient Ischemic Attack (TIA), which is a minor stroke, and requested permission to provide treatment. The treatment was crucial, and time was of the essence. I agreed to the treatment. Then they discovered, upon the completion of an MRI, that he had a large blood clot on the left side of his brain, and they needed to medivac him to The University of Maryland in downtown Baltimore to have it removed immediately.

Because I knew I was going to be at the hospital for some time, I had my daughter take me home to change clothes. My thoughts were overwhelmed with how surgery would go. While at home the surgeon from The University of Maryland called requesting authorization to perform the surgical procedure to remove the blood clot from Sam's brain; of course, I obliged. I was experiencing an array of emotions - mainly disbelief - about what was happening. I felt myself operating on autopilot and feared the unknown. I had never had anyone close to me so critically sick. I was trying to keep myself from breaking down and in doing so it took some time before I allowed myself to feel anything.

When we arrived at the hospital, the procedure was over. Sam was unconscious in intensive care (ICU), on life support. The neurosurgeon came in to speak with me to let me know that my husband did not have a minor stroke but a critically massive stroke that they diagnosed as terminal. I looked at the doctor and said, "Absolutely not! This can't be." It was well after midnight, and I sat in a chair beside his bed and wondered what was going on. One week we were celebrating an anniversary and now the doctor was telling me I may be planning a funeral. It was not making sense to me at all.

I began praying and asking God - what is this! I needed answers. One reason that I have a prayer life is because this helps me to determine what is happening. Conversations with God is often the catalyst for peace in situations that do not yield peace. I immediately reverted back to the conversation I had with God about me marrying Sam. For some reason I had to remind myself that God had released me to enter this marriage. For me this was important because at the time that Sam had the stroke, we had just celebrated two years of marriage and I could not believe that God would allow me to marry him and take him from me after two years. And once I was reminded about that exchange, I was back to asking - what is this. By now I have prayed, a host of other family and friends are praying, and within myself I feel like everything was going to be alright. I felt God there with us and I kept saying to Him as long as you are with us, I know that we are good. And I was talking about His manifested presence because He is always with us. I needed to feel Him in that moment which was my peace!

One particularly important lesson that I have learned from my spiritual dad, Archbishop R. L. Dennis, was not to blame everything on the devil. Surely sickness and disease come from him, however God has to authorize the enemy to impact our lives. My husband and I are believers.

We have faith in God; but did not know our faith would increase tremendously because of this test. Also, when I go through things, I tend to make assessments to make sure no sin had caused this to fall on us. Are we in right standing with God? After doing all my checks, we are good with God. Listen, we are not perfect but whatever we struggle with has already been submitted to God. We are covered. So again, what was this? I must have asked God this question a thousand times before I was able to approach the situation. Although I understood, it would take our faith in God as a healer to see Him miraculously move on Sam's behalf.

As the morning rose upon us, I was approached by a gang of white coated doctors, ranging from neurosurgeons to neurologists, and the primary doctor on Sam's case, Dr. Moss. They wanted to meet with me about what was occurring medically with him. Their approach was very matter-of-fact with little bedside manner. I had no idea what I was about to hear. As I reflect on the situation, I was more prepared for that moment than I believed initially.

They informed me that my husband had suffered a massive left-brain stroke that affected his right side. The left-brain stroke impacted his speech and his ability to move and function on the right side. The doctors had no hesitancy advising me that Sam would not survive that type of stroke. Yes, they were talking death. The blood clot in his brain had caused damage that turned into major swelling. To prevent his brain from crushing his skull due to that pressure, they could remove a portion of his skull. They asked if I wanted them to perform the surgery although his chances of surviving were exceptionally low. At one point, they quoted that he had a ten percent chance of living. He would die within four months. And if he survived, they said, he would be in a nursing home requiring assistance with feeding, dressing and he would be unable to speak.

My decision was in favor of the surgery to remove his skull so that he could live. They further advised the surgery would not reverse the damage caused by the stroke and wanted to ensure that I understood that death was possible. I certainly understood that nothing additionally could be done to help my husband; I relied on my faith in God's power to reverse the damage from the stroke to heal him in ways that doctors were unable. When I spoke about my faith in God, the lead physician seemed to grow frustrated with me which caused me to become increasingly frustrated with her. I reminded her of two important points: she does not have the authority over life or death and was limited in her knowledge and wisdom. However, God is not limited in wisdom or knowledge. My faith is in Him and His ability to move in this place! They made their point, and I made my point. Our God reigns even in this, and He will get glory no matter what He decides to do. I was not good on the inside although I knew we were in a fight for his life.

The surgery was performed, and a portion of Sam's skull was removed. His brain swelled. This was not cute at all, and I don't mean cosmetically. The entire situation was horrible. To watch him swell in that manner, then have to wait for the swelling to subside before they were able to be clear on how much damage was caused by the stroke. It felt like the medical team, and I were on opposing teams, as if they wanted to see him die. They declared what they thought would be so. And I wanted him to live so that they would understand that God has the final say over my husband (His son's) life. God certainly would cause us to be victorious!

The first couple of days after the surgery he remained unconscious and on life support. I found encouragement in knowing he was breathing 80 percent on his own. I read Psalms 118:17 and other scriptures over Sam multiple times daily. I would pray until heaven came down. I was full spiritually and believed God for total recovery for Sam. Although I had not experienced anything like this before in my life, I have gone through other challenges where

I had to exercise my faith against all odds. During those times, I watched God turn things around in His timing. Although the experience was different for me, God is the same God. The word of God reminds us that He changes not in Malachi 3:6. He can do anything but fail. I looked at those doctors knowing we would see who would win this battle.

In the meantime, I continued to pray and believe God along with a host of other people. Both my husband and I are loved by many praying people. The prayers of the righteous avails much power and we were living off of those prayers. As I continued to pray, they continued to bring discouraging news. The news fueled me to pray harder and believe more. It attempted to wear me down; spiritual warfare was high!

They performed neurological tests daily. Initially Sam was responsive, then one day things made a turn for the worse. He was not responding to any commands, which meant that his brain cells were dead. The doctors took me into a room to show me, on screen, how his brain cells had been injured. The results looked bad; I refused to succumb to that report. I proclaimed that I cannot receive what the scans show, what the test results displayed. This was all a test and God will show Himself on our behalf. God told me this is for His glory. My response was that we are moving forward with surgery because he is going to live and not die. There was a time when the doctor and I argued because she was accusing me of being selfish by wanting Sam to live even if he was not going to live a decent quality of life. My response to her was not to worry about his quality of life. God was in control. I constantly reminded the doctor that she was not the giver or taker of life. Despite her god-complex, she was NOT the ultimate healer.

After having several interactions of this manner with her she started avoiding me, which was fine with me. She did not have anything good to say anyway and I was tired of hearing her reports. I was frustrated with the entire experience and having to hear this news repeatedly was not good for me. It was hard to hear and emotionally it was draining. Initially it was important for me to hear the medical team's diagnosis as well as the prognosis for Sam's condition, how else would I know what I needed to petition God for on his behalf. So, once I heard it there was no other reason for me to continue to subject myself to hearing that repeatedly. In fact, no matter how many times the medical team was determined to speak it that had no impact on what I was believing God to do for my husband. The Bible clearly says faith comes by hearing and hearing by the Word of God. I had to keep speaking the word of God that specifically spoke to my present situation if I wanted to see and hear something different from the medical team. The medical team kept speaking death and I continued to proclaim Psalms 118:17 (MSG). "I didn't die. I lived! And now I'm telling the world what God did, which is the word that God gave me." I proclaimed this scripture until I saw things begin to change and nothing spoken or seen deterred me.

This continued on for about two weeks before they discovered Sam was a retired veteran, so they transferred him to the VA hospital, with a new medical team. This medical team conducted medical assessments of Sam and scheduled a meeting with the immediate family; so, we met. In the meeting, I was already on the defensive ready to battle whatever they had to say. As you can imagine I am both physically and spiritually exhausted. The medical team, about 20 in number, comprised of neurologists, surgeons, nurses, general practitioners, and a social worker sat us down to give their report. The report was the same as the one from the medical team at University Hospital; he would die and if he lived, he would not live beyond four months. If he lived longer, he would be in a vegetative state requiring daily living assistance. In fact, they were preparing to have him transferred to an assisted living facility. It was quite a bit to take in and in a brief period. It was all happening so quickly, and I was living between no, this was not happening and really, God!

I refused to accept the reports. The devil is a liar, and I would not trust in what he wanted me to! The God I serve loves me and is concerned about everything that is a concern for me. That's what was shouting in my spirit. Sam's mother responded before I could say anything; she asked the medical team, "not to give up on my son because we were believing God to heal him." The doctor's response was quite different from the previous physician at the university. He said, "you are right, and I do apologize everyone is different." I am not sure what he meant by his response, but he seemed open to the possibility that things could change. This medical team had some understanding of their human limitations and acknowledged our faith that God was in control and would take on our matter. That was exactly what happened!

During the first week, Sam still had not responded positively. The neurologist gave him commands, like Sam raise your hand. Sam looked at him as if he were speaking a foreign language. I did not allow that to persuade me otherwise, I continued believing God and encouraged Sam to fight for his life. On the 29th day in the ICU, there was an awakening, manifestation of a move of God. The neurologist came into the room to give Sam his commands for that day. He said, "Sam move your finger" and Sam raised his left arm. Prior to this response Sam had given no indication that he understood anything that was spoken to him. As the doctor turned to leave the room, he looked at Sam and smiled while saying, "You are going to make a liar out of me." And his mother responded, "he sure is!" As the days passed, we began to see more improvement, so much so that one of the previous doctors responded to me by saying, "No way, this is unfreakingbelievable!" And my response to him was I told you all that God was going to heal him, and he responded, "you sure did." Sweet victory in Jesus! Although we still had a long way to go, we had a notable miracle in progress. YES! Miracles, signs, and wonders follow them that believe God! Our faith was making us whole.

Shortly after that and with more progression the medical team had to change the direction that they were initially moving in which was trying to find an assisted living facility for Sam to spend the remainder of his days requiring 24-hour care. God had other plans. One day one of the nurses came to me prior to them transferring Sam from ICU to a regular floor. She informed me about the Hunter Holmes McGuire VA Medical Center in Richmond, Virginia where they had a polytrauma rehabilitation floor in the hospital. The facility is a state-of-the-art facility with all the needed equipment and qualified medical team well experienced with working with individuals with brain injuries such as what Sam experienced. There are only five of these VA programs in the country and this one was the closest in proximity to where we lived. She said, "your husband is young and that his best chances for maximum recovery would be him going to this facility." Without hesitation I made the decision for Sam to go to the facility in Richmond, so they started the process to get him admitted. In the meantime, I had to speak with my employer; but they had already extended grace because of the favor of God. I was permitted to work remotely from Richmond. The Fisher House, for veteran's family members to reside without cost while family member was in the hospital offered five-star accommodations. That was particularly important to me. It confirmed for me that God had the minute details already worked out for us. During the entire journey, we experienced nothing but the favor of God. His hand was in it from the beginning, and I rested in the belief that this experience was going to work out for our good. As I think back the fact that Sam made it off Interstate 95 without an accident, made it home, and for an angel in our neighborhood to find him, meant, surely God is engaged in the matter!!!

We were three months into the journey and off to Richmond we went. We would be there for four additional months. I was emotionally drained and exhausted, but I felt like we were moving forward, God was with us, and we were going to be good. From October to January, Sam was in The Polytrauma Center, and I was at The Fisher House. His rehabilitation occurred during 8 a.m. to 4 p.m., so I visited him daily afterward and remained at the hospital through dinner; Most days he was exhausted because of the rigorous therapy plan they had for him. The schedule worked for me because during the day I was working, and when I left him in the evening, I was able to get schoolwork completed. Yes, in the midst of all that was happening I was in the dissertation phase of my doctoral degree.

As a routine I would drive home every week to check on our house, get my hair done and work onsite to ensure that things were good. The next day I would return to Richmond at the end of Sam's therapy sessions for the day. Along with the medical team there we established goals for Sam to achieve and he continued making great strides on his way to becoming independent. The therapist worked him hard every day and he gave it all 110 percent. Sam displayed enthusiasm like they had never seen which was inspiring to the staff and other patients. He would sing to them, and they enjoyed it. It was amazing. I was stunned to learn that singing used a different part of your brain which is different from the portion used for speech.

Sam was able to learn how to walk again. I was grateful, especially because getting the wheelchair and him in and out of the car was horrible for me. I cried every time. I am so glad that God released us from that. Sam was incredibly determined to walk. The VA wanted to put a ramp on the house for the wheelchair before they would allow him to come home. I remember the day they met with us in the hospital and asked if they could install the wheelchair ramp. Sam said no emphatically, and we all turned to look at him because he was not very vocal prior to this moment. The VA informed us that they had to install it, or they would not approve him to come home. We scheduled the date to have it installed. By the time that date arrived, Sam was walking. We canceled that installation. Thank you, Jesus!

Sam came home for Christmas for a break until the New Year and then returned to Richmond for the transitional rehabilitation program that he was accepted into. The program was an additional four months of rehabilitation. We were excited but we had to endure the first visit home without all the medical team to assist Sam and me. It was all me and I soon learned that my new role for my husband was caretaker, and I was not prepared! My thoughts were stating for richer or poorer and in sickness and health. I remember thinking we were declaring restored health as we continued on the path. I remember asking God why we couldn't have been married for 20 or more years before encountering such a significant battle. I wondered why He did not allow us to build a longer foundation first; then I realized that this was a part of our foundation, and we would still be building this on a solid rock.

When we were preparing to return home, we met with the pharmacist to get Sam's medication list. I promise that it seemed as if my husband must have been on more than 30 medications. I had been so emotional. Jesus, why does he have to take all these medications? The pharmacist assured me that he would be weaned off most of it. Why did they tell me that? Every week I was asking the doctors what medicines were we coming off each week? Yes, I was also my husband's advocate. He was not going to keep taking all that medication. He was being healed in Jesus' name. Little by little, the medication decreased. Physically, Sam was making progress, but his speech was progressing slowly. He was able to speak what I now know to be automatic language, such as inquiring how are you. His struggle was language expression and at times comprehension, which is called global aphasia. I had never heard of global aphasia prior to this experience.

We came home for the Christmas holiday, which is my favorite holiday. That Christmas was a special one after all that we had been through. I promise you there is a God and I know that He is right here with us. We hosted Christmas dinner for both our families, and it was wonderful. My family teased me because I had multiple celebrations for Sam; and I was going to continue to celebrate the miracle man of mine for the rest of our lives.

When Sam returned to University of Maryland Hospital to have cranioplasty surgery, I was anxious. I wanted so badly to see the doctors who proclaimed death and not walking or talking for Sam. I wanted them to see that victory belongs to Jesus and He always delivers. Once we arrived, the surgeon came into the room looking as if he had seen a ghost. He was surprised to see Sam in this condition. He sent for some of the other members of the original medical team so they could witness how much Sam had progressed. One of the neurologists said, "I don't think I have ever seen anyone recover from such a massive stroke in this manner." I said that God was going to do it and He is not finished yet. We will be back, and his response was "sometimes you get it right and sometimes you get it wrong." I know he did not want to believe God did this. He would rather admit that he got it wrong and either way it spoke to his limitations as a physician. He owed it to himself and his patients to seek a source higher than his level of wisdom and knowledge. It was good to see them and hopefully our experience has taught them something that will cause them to consider God in what they do.

The cranioplasty surgery went well. After Sam recovered from surgery, he returned to Richmond to the Polytrauma Transitional Rehabilitation Program which was the next step in his recovery plan. Six months had passed. And although we were not sure how much longer the road would be, we still believed God. We continued to speak the Word of God and He would have the final say over our situation and circumstances. While Sam was in the program, they only allowed me to stay for the first two weeks because they did not want family interfering with that level of treatment. His treatment embarked on something new, such as getting him prepared to live on his own if he had to. This also gave me an opportunity to rest and replenish myself which was desperately needed. After six months, I was expecting the journey to end at any moment, but God had another plan. The longer it was, the more worn down I became. I started to dislike what I was seeing in the mirror because the exhaustion was evident. I had never experienced anything like this in my life before. I had never seen anyone in my family as a caretaker. This was a role far from what my resume indicated I was capable of, I assure you.

As a caretaker, you are intercessor and everything else that may be required.

Four months into treatment, Sam was making great strides in all areas of rehabilitation except for speech. Was there a conspiracy against his speech progression? I wondered why the physical therapists were highly trained in every facility we received treatment, but the same was not the case for speech therapists. They could not seem to provide what he needed. My husband was diagnosed with global aphasia. In laymen's terms, global aphasia was worst case scenario, and the prognosis was there was no return from it, absolutely no healing. They reported that his speech would not return to normal. My belief was this would not be the case. When God performed His miracle, no one would be able to say anything other than the miraculous. We chose to continue to wait and believe God for it! Sam did those four months and returned home for a break. And yes, you got it, I had another coming home celebration for Sam.

During his time home, he received speech and physical therapy twice weekly; still the speech therapist did not seem to have the skill level to assist Sam. With no progression in speech, we ended that therapy, which was disappointing for both Sam and me. Sam not being able to communicate created challenges in our marriage and increased struggle to believe that he would be healed. Physical therapy reported that he had progressed to his maximum capacity for their environment. At this point, he was fully independent. Even though we are not at total restoration, we are a great distance from where we started and far from the diagnosis. Sadly, what I discovered is that far too many in the medical field (at least on our path) have low or no expectations of people getting healed beyond a certain level of care. The medical field needs sick people in its system to prosper; and I get it, but we would not be a part of that.

So, Sam had been home for a year, and he no longer wanted to be away from home. Although he was independent, he could not be left alone because he was not able to communicate if an emergency occurred. So, part of the week, my parents came to stay with us. The other days Sam went to his aunt's house. That got tiring after a while for all parties involved. So, we decided that it was time to return to Richmond for additional rehabilitation, especially speech. I placed a call for a return visit, and he returned for only 14 weeks this time. During the 14 weeks, there was absolutely no progress made. As long as there was progress, Sam could stay in the program until he reached his goals. With no progress, Sam was discharged. In the discharge meeting, the therapist gave reports and were saying that Sam had the words in his brain because he was able to repeat words. However, he was not retaining the words. They also reported that he could not move his right arm because it was not making a connection to the command center - his brain. It did not discourage me. I felt as soon as God was ready to release this it was going to happen. Everything that was needed to make it happen was there. We needed the miraculous to occur in the brain and God can do it. We returned home, and I believe Sam was disappointed in not making any progress this time. Things had been tough from my perspective; I couldn't begin to imagine his inner turmoil. But I was encouraged knowing what our result would be. God's timing is not our timing. As we wait for our expected end, our declaration remains for total healing and restoration. God always does exceedingly and abundantly above all we can ask or think.

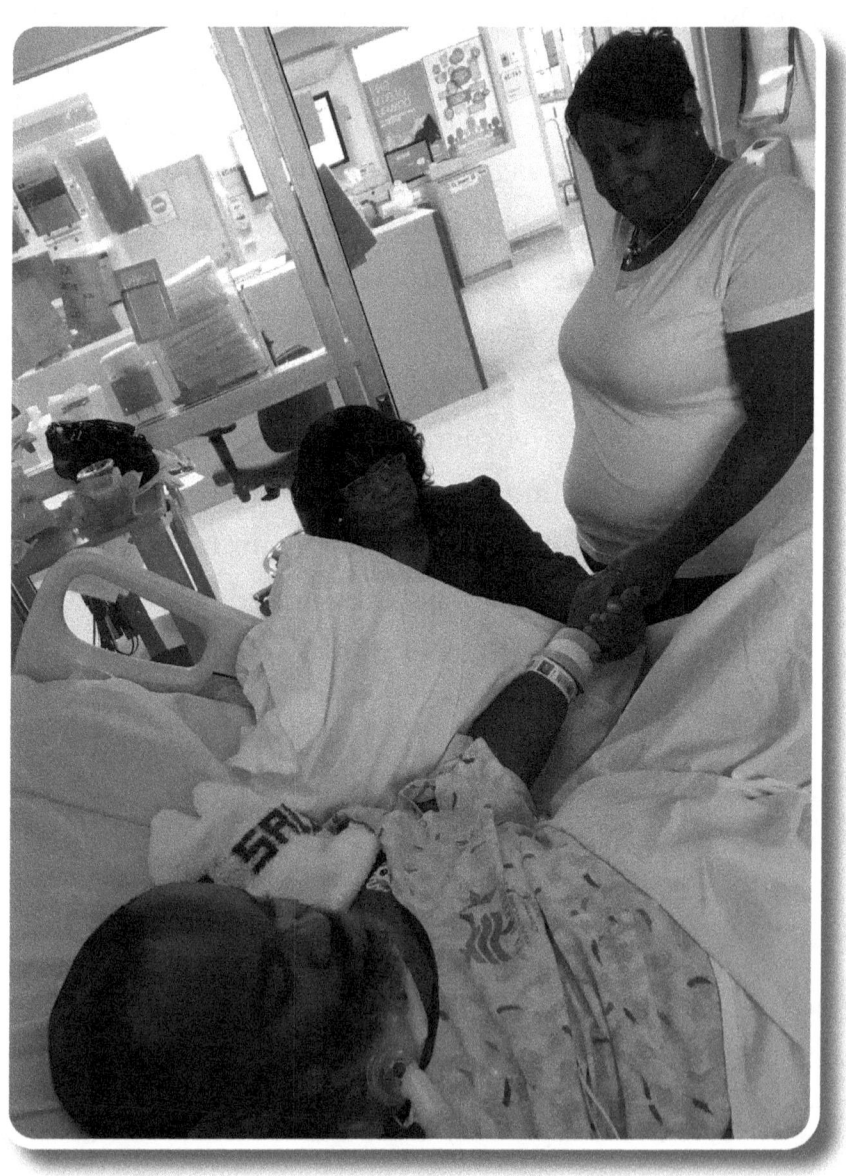

CHAPTER 4

Making Sense of Faith

NOTHING ABOUT FAITH MAKES sense. The Bible declares in Hebrews 11:1 that faith is the substance of things hoped for and the evidence of things not seen. Who hopes for things that you can't see? Well as believers we are all called to have hope in things that we cannot see with the natural eyes. However, it is through our faith that we can in time see them unfold with our natural eyes. We must train ourselves to see it before we actually see it! It is in seeing it that we will be able to see it. See what I mean? It does not make sense, but faith is our fundamental truth as believers. God has given us faith to be able to make the transfer between what we are hoping for even when there is no evidence. It seems to be challenging sometimes until we come to a crossroads in our relationship with God where we have seen enough of Him to have grown in our faith for what seems impossible. As believers we should always exercise our faith in

God. There are enough impossibilities in life to keep us turning our wheels for faith for life. We all know people who we believe have great faith and we watch them face impossibility after impossibility. We witness impossibilities become possible and are amazed. We can all experience this kind of manifestation in our lives by having the same kind of faith in God.

The Bible declares in Romans 10:17 that faith comes by hearing and hearing by the word of God. If we are desiring to increase our faith, we must spend time listening to and reading the word of God. This is how we learn more about who God is and that will increase our confidence in His ability and increase our understanding in His love for us. We must resist the temptation to doubt and not trust God. The way to achieve this is through His word. He has established Himself through His word and has demonstrated this in our lives enough to show that His track record is exemplary. For this very reason once the medical team explained what was going on with my husband, I had no reason to accept their prognosis because that could cause me to doubt what God's word says about healing. In Isaiah 53:5 the word of God says by His stripes we are healed and as believers we have to believe God's word. I exercised my faith and decided to rely on God's word because that is what I believe for healing. I declared life while they spoke death, and had I allowed them to overshadow my faith that could not have been a possibility. We do not want to ignore what the reality is because that would not be wise but after you have a full understanding of what is transpiring then as believers God has given us a prescribed method on how we should operate. We need to understand that there will be opposition especially when we decide to have faith and trust God in another dimension. We can be assured that opposition will come to discourage us, and we must be determined to be encouraged despite what the adversary tries to bring against us. We have the assurance of knowing that our faith in God who is all-knowing will move on our behalf without fail. Faith does not mean that God always does what we want Him to do. Our faith must be matured in God and must know that God is God regardless of what He decides to do. And I remind myself that if God had decided to allow Sam's life in those moments that this did not translate that God is not good. God is good whether things turn out how we desire and when they do not. That requires a certain level of maturity in God otherwise we become angry with God when things do not turn out how we desire them too. God is not our magician to move on our every beck and call. However, He is our loving Father who has a plan and purpose for our lives. When the enemy comes against that He will do battle on our behalf. This flows out of our relationship with God and without it, life is more challenging than it needs to be.

We should surrender and submit to God's will for our lives and understand this is not about our plan for our life. When we view God as the creator that He is, we understand that His intent for our lives is more important than any plans that we could ever desire. Our trust for Him allows us to seek Him for His plan and surrender to that plan also. After seeking and receiving revelation, be obedient to what He is requiring. It takes courage to be obedient. Reliance upon God and knowing He cares for us and the things that are a concern for us allows it to become easier. The more we mature in God the more we seek His will and desire understanding that to be the most important.

Our maturity also causes us to be able to rest assuredly in God because we understand he has us. In past times I have wondered how some people endured tumultuous times and had profound peace that only comes from resting in God. Most times in this journey I have been able to rest in God. And the times that I became anxious and unsure were the times I was relying on myself and not resting in God. Some of my own anxiety was due to me wanting things to happen according to my timeline, as well as not fully understanding that God knows what He is doing. And even when I could not see Him moving, it did not mean that He was not moving. What do we do as we wait is really determined by our perception? In most cases, during the delay God is silent What is our response to the silence? What does the delay mean? Everything is determined by our interpretation of the two. How we define them dictates how we respond or even our lack of response.

What we think is a delay is God moving according to His timing, not ours, because He is in control. If not cautioned in the delay, we sometimes allow doubt to overshadow us and then fear and anxiety creeps in. It is crucial to remain in faith and rest in God knowing that what we believe God for will happen despite what happens in the meantime. Make sure you are connected to people who have faith. Sometimes it can be difficult. We all have different measures of faith. This journey has been interesting when I speak what we are believing God for to some believers. Their responses have been intriguing to say the least. When nonbelievers respond with disbelief, that is the appropriate response. However, when people who proclaim to know God respond in this manner, it is mind blowing. No matter how mind blowing this is, it has not persuaded me to believe what God can do. I note it and move forward. It is key for you to know what you believe no matter who stands with you. On some days you may stand alone and that will have to be enough. Stand firm at all costs. Stand in faith believing and your faith will deliver that which you believed for in accordance with God's Plan. Your faith may cost you relationships. It may cause isolation. If God is with you, this is a good place for you to be. God knows what you need and when you need it.

Let's discuss sensory perception versus faith. We are so accustomed to living in the natural. If things do not measure up to our sense, we find them hard to believe. Meaning if we are not able to see it with our eyes, feel it through touch, smell it, hear it, or taste it, this poses a problem for some of us. As believers, we are called upon to be spiritual beings and live our lives spiritually discerning things versus naturally discerning them.

Faith is not faith until it's been tested. This statement is absolutely true. We make declarations and proclaim ourselves as believers. When life happens, and it happens to us all, our response will be the determining factor as to how much faith really exist. God does allow situations to occur in our lives to increase our faith even in times when we feel like it is a lot to bear. We discover that strength was in us all along. God knows what He has placed inside of us, and we are more prepared for the battle than we know. However, we do find that to be the case in the end. God also knows what kind of pressure is required to bring it out of us. This is not the kinds of things we like to discuss but God does allow us to be crushed and His intent is never to harm us but to bring out of us that which He placed inside of us. In those times, faith is required because we may become angry with God for allowing this to happen. I know I am speaking truth because in my own life I have had to pray asking God to keep my heart from hardening, especially when we consider God can prevent it all. This does not mature and grow us in Him. He is concerned about those things that concern us but more importantly about our development in Him. There will be pain that He will not spare us from, although He is more than able. For some people that is a hard pill to swallow.

I remember being in a horrible place as it relates to Sam being sick. I pushed my way through it. I attended worship and I remember hearing someone say, who worships a God who will not finish the miracle. I thought it was a great question. As I continued on through this journey, my answer to that question is that He is not finished yet. Without faith, I am done! This is my understanding of faith making me whole. Most days I understood that without faith in God I was a disaster waiting to happen which is what the enemy wanted. The enemy of my soul wanted not only to kill Sam but destroy me in any way that he could which made me that much more determined to lean on God, especially on the hard days. All I have is my faith and that is all we need to see the manifestation of our miracle. And I promise you that God is faithful. Miracles happen every day! For those who believe that God does not perform miracles in our present time, shame on you. For me, I want to continue to see the manifestation of miracles, and I have the faith by Almighty God to see them transpire. Yes, He equipped me for this journey. As stated previously, I was equipped more than I fully understood. You never go through things without coming out on the other side of it changed. My convictions are stronger, and faith has been endowed. I am more committed to believing God and encouraging those who have lost faith or belief in God to have the courage to believe and have faith again!!!

Miracles, signs, and wonders follow the people that believe, and we believe God and, in the miracles, signs and wonders that follow us. Miracles are the temporary suspension of the natural order of events or the reversal of natural laws. Nature has laws that are set in motion that when certain things occur, other things follow. God has supernatural laws that at His ordering can and will cause an interruption to the natural law. We never fully understand how it happens. Those are the mysteries of God. I do not want to just read about the miracles that are written in the word of God I want to be used of God for Him to perform the miraculous in the Earth realm today causing others to believe in Him.

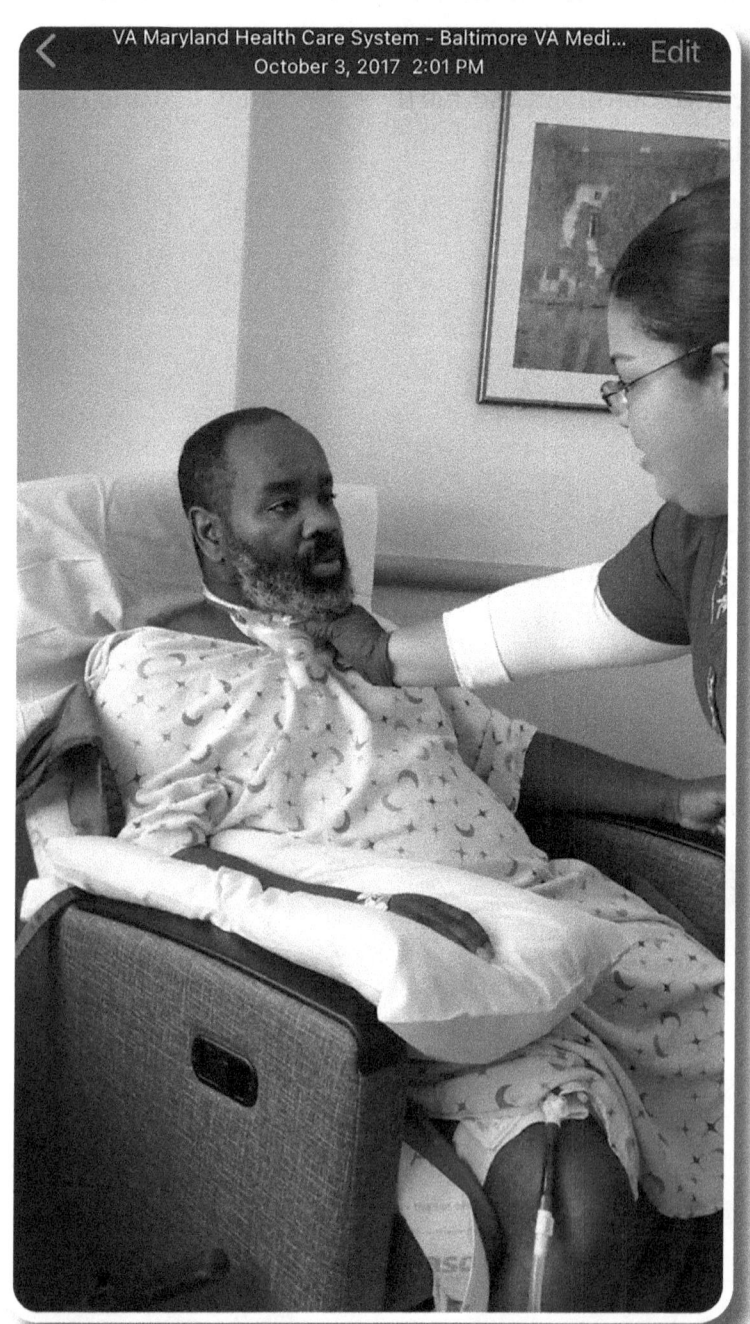

CHAPTER FIVE

I Have Found Grace to be Amazing!

IT WAS GOD'S GRACE! His grace is everything! I have found grace to be amazing. The Bible declares that God's grace is sufficient, and I have found that to be true. When I was immature in my faith, I believed grace was God's way of covering our sins. As I matured in Him, I discovered that when I received His sanctifying grace it provided me with the strength not to live in sin. Then as I matured even more, I learned that with grace comes enabling power and strength to get things accomplished, which is serving grace. Whatever assignment or task that God was requiring of me, I now understand that I had the grace to complete the task. It makes difficult things appear effortless.

I am confident that the grace of God and His favor rest on my life in ways that unfolded along this journey. The fact that I was able to make it through and remain sane despite the internal crushing that I felt in my spirit - was His grace. My husband came close to death after only two years of marriage and that weighed on my psyche. I realized that there have been wives who have buried husbands in less time than that, and my prayers are extended to them. This provided further understanding that it was His grace. Even the fact that I had become his caretaker, caused me to grab hold to God's grace, and I found it every time I needed it.

I was able to keep everything flowing with my job, even my coworkers were amazed. In addition, I was able to complete my doctoral degree even though my dissertation chairperson suggested that I take a semester or two off. I had a push on the inside of me that kept me pressing and I was glad that I did. When I walked across the stage to get that degree, I knew that God had ordained this very thing for my life because it was His grace that kept me pushing through it all. My husband suffered the stroke only 45 days after we settled on our new home. We lost income and were still able to pay all of our bills on time. This was the grace and favor of God. I was able to decorate our new home during the process. The retail therapy helped me as well. God's hand is on both Sam's and my life. God orchestrated our introduction and union.

Today I am clearer about that than I have ever been. The fact that I have felt His hand involved in the entire journey gave me strength to continue even during the bad days, and there have been many. The grace of God covered me and for this I am grateful! I assure you there were days that I felt like I almost lost my mind. It was His grace that would not allow me to lose it because He had a plan for us. We moved forward in that journey despite what the enemy had tried to do. It has not and did not prosper. And because of His grace, this will all work out for our good. We are witnesses in the Earth of a gracious God, who shows mercy to those whom He chooses.

Now I know why the psalmist sang Amazing grace because it certainly is and has been amazing in my life. This journey has been awful and amazing all at the same time. It was awful that we had to experience it all, but we have been able to know God in new ways because of this experience. He had been gracious because others believed that I was going to bury my husband, but God's grace and mercy kept us moving right forward. I kept reminding myself that we were passing through this place. We are not staying here. As we continued to progress, I kept saying it was His grace keeping us. Yes, the grace of God has keeping power along with the ability to accomplish the unthinkable. Grace is undeserved favor from God in the simplest form He is merciful!

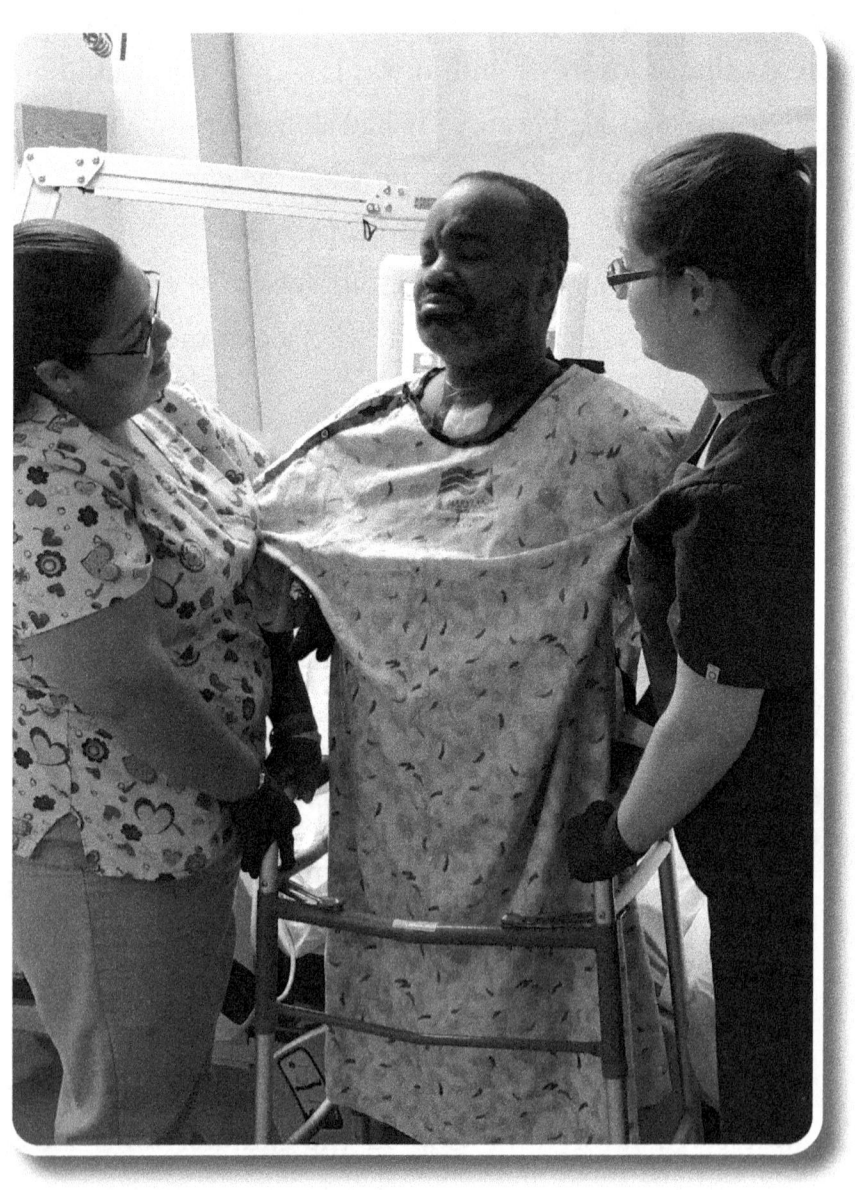

CHAPTER 6

New Things Spring Up

Isaiah 43:18-19

Forget about the former things. I'm doing something new. Don't you perceive it or know it?

Many of us feel like we know God based on how He has moved previously in our lives. Those experiences with Him cause us to become familiar with who He is and how He operates; however, we really only know God based on the experiences we have had with Him. In the same manner that we became familiar with our family, friends, and others. Experiences impact who God is in our lives. For instance, if you have experienced sickness and God has healed you, you know God to be a healer. If you have experienced the provision of God, then you come to know Him as a provider. All the knowledge that we have about God is based on our occurrences. The more we experience with Him, the more we grow and mature in our understanding of Him. God uses challenges in our lives, such as the things that the enemy throws our way to cause us to stumble, and the challenges that we have caused in our own lives to mature us in Him. He desires for us to know Him more intimately. With every level of challenge, we become more familiar.

We do not fully know God. We sometimes resist getting to know God in new ways because we have become complacent in our familiarity with God. We become accustomed to how He moved in previous times in our lives and that gives us a certain level of comfort. We become relaxed, even though we know there is so much more to whom God is. It is something about us being comfortable and not really wanting to be stretched although we declare that we want to go to the next level. Our actions rarely align. Instead of having an experience like Peter in the boat with God, in which he called out to Jesus asking to be called out of the boat and onto the water. This is uncomfortable for some of us. We would rather remain in a place that is safe. I am acquainted with this position of comfort. Being comfortable brings us a certain level of peace and places us at ease because we feel like we have a certain level of control over situations. In familiar situations, we assume that we know the outcome and that gives us a certain level of assurance which is contrary to faith. Peter had another level kind of faith in God, not knowing what would happen after he stepped out of the boat. He had confidence that Jesus would keep him safe even if the experience were a new one. He was willing to move forward, to know and learn something different about who Jesus was.

God desires to do a new thing in us all. The question that He asks is do you perceive what I am trying to do in your life now that is different from times in past? God desires for us to know Him; and in knowing Him, we must have new and different experiences that will often be uncomfortable and unfamiliar. The new thing that God desires to do in us will challenge, stretch, and mature us in ways we have not formerly known. God has a purpose for the stretching that will not be experienced in our comfort zones.

It is fear and anxiety that prevents us from desiring the new things that God wants to do. The unfamiliar makes you extremely uncomfortable. We do not like being uncomfortable even if it is to get to the next level. We want to reach our goals effortlessly. We want to stay in the comfort zone because it is safe. We tell ourselves that we are not sure what the unfamiliar will cost us but knowing that it will cost us something. However, it is the price that we pay in exchange for a new experience with God, which is priceless. It will cost us some relationships, reputation, finances, some wills, and desires but the trade-off is allowing God to have His way in our lives which should be our focus in life. What God exchanges in our lives for the sacrifices that we make is really an uneven exchange and for that we should be grateful.

What are we afraid of? God is constantly beckoning us to greater because He knows that it is inside of us. He placed it there; nevertheless, we desire to remain in a place of comfort when there is so much unfamiliar territory to cover with God.

To say we know God is a limited concept we know Him only according to our last experience with Him. He desires our knowing of Him to be ever growing and expanding. The Bible declares that His depth is so deep, and His width is so wide that there is a lot of Him to discover. This journey is all planned and designed by Him for us. All we must do is be willing to follow Him into unfamiliar territory, which makes most of us extremely uncomfortable. We must have the courage to go with Him even if we are afraid. The more experiences we have with Him increases our faith and trust in Him knowing that He has us and all that concerns us.

The Father is always bidding us to seek Him, and that door is open to us constantly. He created us in this fashion but somehow, we have allowed other desires that we believe to be more pertinent than the desire to seek Him a priority. Somehow, He gets placed after everything else when our main focus in life should be our relationship with Him. In this we discover that if we seek Him, we could avoid chasing after things that are not for our lives.

We seek to know a lot of things and people that we think will advance our cause. But the only person we need to seek to know more of is God, who is a master at making the connections that we need with the right people far better than we could ever. We seem to think that we know what is best for our lives better than the One who created us in His image and for His purpose. We need to lean in and pursue Him more than we are cognizant of. We have wasted time trying to figure out our own lives when there is already a master blueprint that we can access. We are trying to figure things out when life could be simpler doing it the way that God designed it.

The psalmist David asked the question: Who are we that You, God, are mindful of us? He knows us. And in our discovering who He is helps us in knowing who we are because we only find that in Him. It is impossible to discover who we are outside of God because who we are is only found in Him. Some of us are on a quest to discover who we are outside of Him. And just as we will not fully know who God is outside of our seeking of Him, we will not become fully aware of who we are until we seek Him.

It is amazing how in seeking Him not only is He revealed but who we are in Him is revealed as well. All that we are, who He created us to be, and our gifts and talents are all wrapped in the One who created us. This is crucial because it shows that we could never be a full expression of ourselves without Him, and we certainly try. We think about how good we think we are which means we could be so much greater seeking Him regularly, not just when we find ourselves in trouble but in advance so that we might not find ourselves in trouble. Our experiences led by Him will sometimes lead us into troubled waters. In our seeking, we discover that He has a plan that leads us through those troubled waters. And the knowledge gained through the process expands once again our knowledge of Him. Knowing Him does not exempt us from trouble; however, knowing Him guarantees our successes and victories with whatever we face.

God loves us and we are not always mindful that He created us for His own pleasure, but we are forever trying to remain on our own agenda instead of following His plan for our lives. It seems that life would be much simpler if we followed His leading, not only when it is convenient but all the time at all costs. We need to know and fully understand that the life that He has designed for us is far greater than anything that we could ever devise ourselves.

Seeking Him would save us so much heartache and frustration along with time. There are traps and snares designed, by the enemy, to look appealing to us. What corrects our view of this ploy of the enemy is seeking God even more and asking Him to allow us to see things for what they really are - traps.

The more we seek God, the more experiences we have with Him and the more we know Him in intimate ways. He is always calling us away to spend time with him. He is always trying to reveal Himself to us in ways we cannot even imagine but it makes us uncomfortable and is frightening for a lot of us. It also makes us feel like we are not in control and that brings anxiety. Therefore, we must trust God even in unfamiliar territory. We have to be confident in His ability to keep us safe through it all. Trusting God comes only through knowing Him and that should be constantly growing. God is forever moving, and we sometimes fail to move with him causing us to miss what He is trying to do in our lives.

We do not want to be where God moved last but where He is moving currently. Where is God trying to take you? What is He trying to do in your life, but you've not trusted in Him enough to make the move into the new? In Isaiah 43, He says, "I will do a new thing; do you not perceive it?" For most of us, we do see it, but it's scary, so instead we pretend like we don't perceive it. Comfort zones are the worst. They cause us to forfeit the new things that God desires to do. We become frustrated about not moving along in life, but it is at our own doing. God is beckoning us into fresh territory but our own will keeps us from moving forward.

Let us make this move together allowing God to have His perfect will in our lives. Sometimes we must allow ourselves to become so desperate for Him that we have enough courage to make the leap into seeking God and following His uniquely designed path for our lives even when things do not appear to be lined up from our perspective.

Let us not be so arrogant to think we know what is best for our lives more than the one who created us. Life would be so much better with a constant flow of seeking and following His leading. We must be mindful that every new level starts in a space that is unfamiliar to us. As we seek God, and He reveals Himself to us, we are learning the new place that God has us in. Sometimes being in that place there is nothing for us to follow from a previous journey, and it can be intimidating. We had confidence in the last place. In the new place, we must become reliant upon God because we do not recognize this place. In the new place, we must surrender and submit to a whole new pattern of being and doing because the old ways will not secure our victory in this new place. God is trying to help us develop new patterns and being in this new place that will yield another dimension in Him causing our faith in Him to unfold displaying things that we have not seen before. Transformation is taking place in this new place and as we come to know God differently another part of who we are is also revealed in this process.

We should be confident in the God that we have surrendered our hearts to knowing that regardless of what He allows life to bring our way, He has a plan. Part of that plan is for us to be victorious on the other side of whatever we are facing. We have to know and believe in our hearts that we always win, and we must be careful of what declarations we make. Assuredly we will have to align our words with our actions. It is time out for saying that I have faith in God but when something happens in life to test that faith there is a great distance between what was declared, and the actions taken. There is a saying that faith is not faith until it has been assessed to be so. As Christians, we destroy our witness when we speak about our faith and during testing times we fall apart. Faith is supposed to be displayed for others to see because that is how we can be great witnesses in the Earth of who God is. He works in and through us and what comes out of our mouth should be aligned with our walk.

As we are walking in this new season we are surrendered and submitted to God for the mission He has for our lives. It is both exciting and fearful. We know God has been and is faithful and that remains to be our declaration despite the road we are traveling. We trust God with all we know and rely on Him for guidance and peace as He leads.

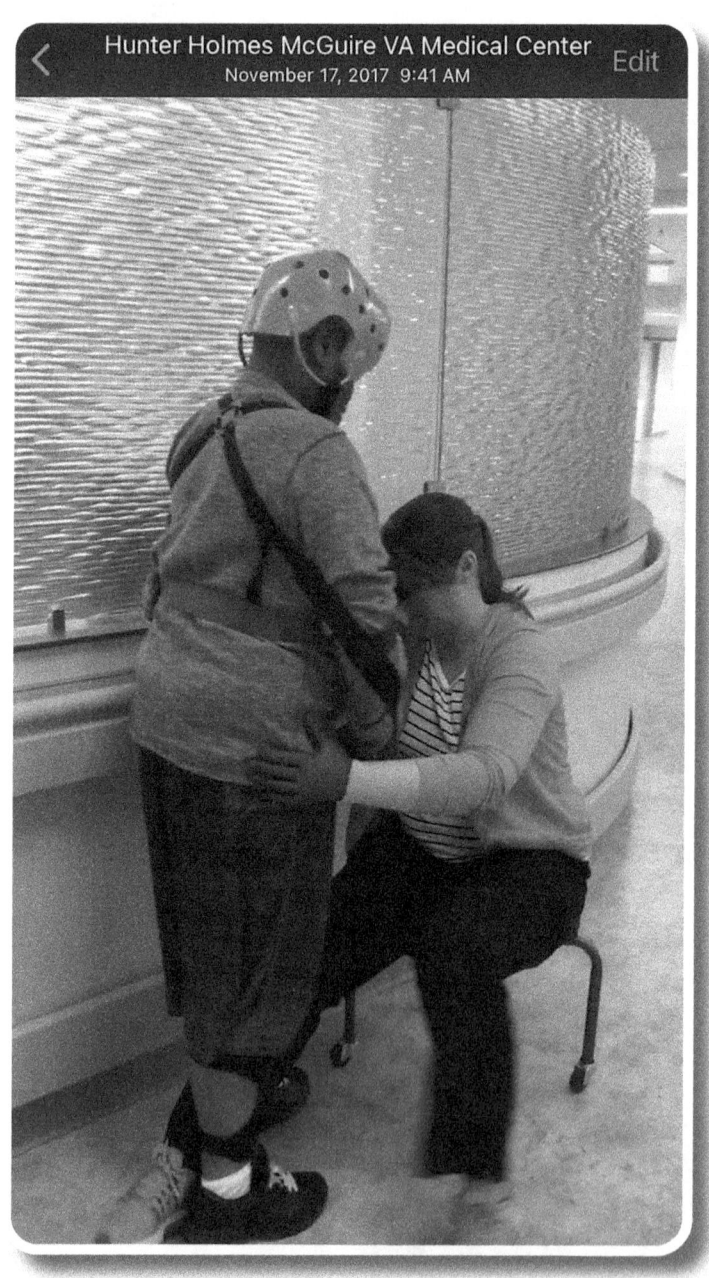

CHAPTER 7

Perfect Conditions

SOMETIMES THINGS ARE NOT always going to seem like the best conditions to start something new, branch out or move into unfamiliar territory. Because of the situation or circumstances, you find yourself in, it may appear that things are over for you, when in reality it really is just the beginning of something new that has been orchestrated by God. It is all about perspective. Sometimes you may want to pack up and call it quits but I want to caution you to look a little closer into who and what is guiding you in the midst of where you are. Occasionally when things seem to be out of order that is the best time to start something new.

While on this journey God has made it clear that He desires to do a new thing in our lives. Even when we thought we were clear about His plans for our lives, we have discovered that He was detouring us off our trajectory and placing us on the map of His plan for our lives. Clearly God has interrupted our lives causing our attention to be fully focused on Him and His desire for our lives. This is what happens when God desires our attention in a new area, an abrupt shift in another direction leading on the path to destiny only designed by Him.

When one considers doing something new or different, it is wise to consider the conditions however let me caution you to consider the conditions differently.

One day while I was watching the funeral of George H. W. Bush, some interesting facts about him were being presented and one that resonated with me is that he was known for using the military acronym CAVU which stands for "ceiling and visibility unlimited." This acronym means perfect flying conditions exist. The orator explained that this was his approach to life. He considers the conditions of things before moving forward. Once I heard this, I could not let it go, or it would not let go of me. From a natural perspective, we can agree that is a logical practice. However, from a spiritual perspective, conditions can only be clear for anyone to move forward when authorized by God. Natural conditions are not necessarily perfect. It is all about your perspective about your situation. Perspective is key and can determine one's outlook on a situation or the circumstances.

As we continue trusting God we move forward in the things of God. Just as the air traffic controller gives the pilots the clearance to take off, it is the same when God determines that now is the time for us to move forward in launching Life Ministry. Spiritually our ceiling and visibility are unlimited, and we have been cleared for takeoff.

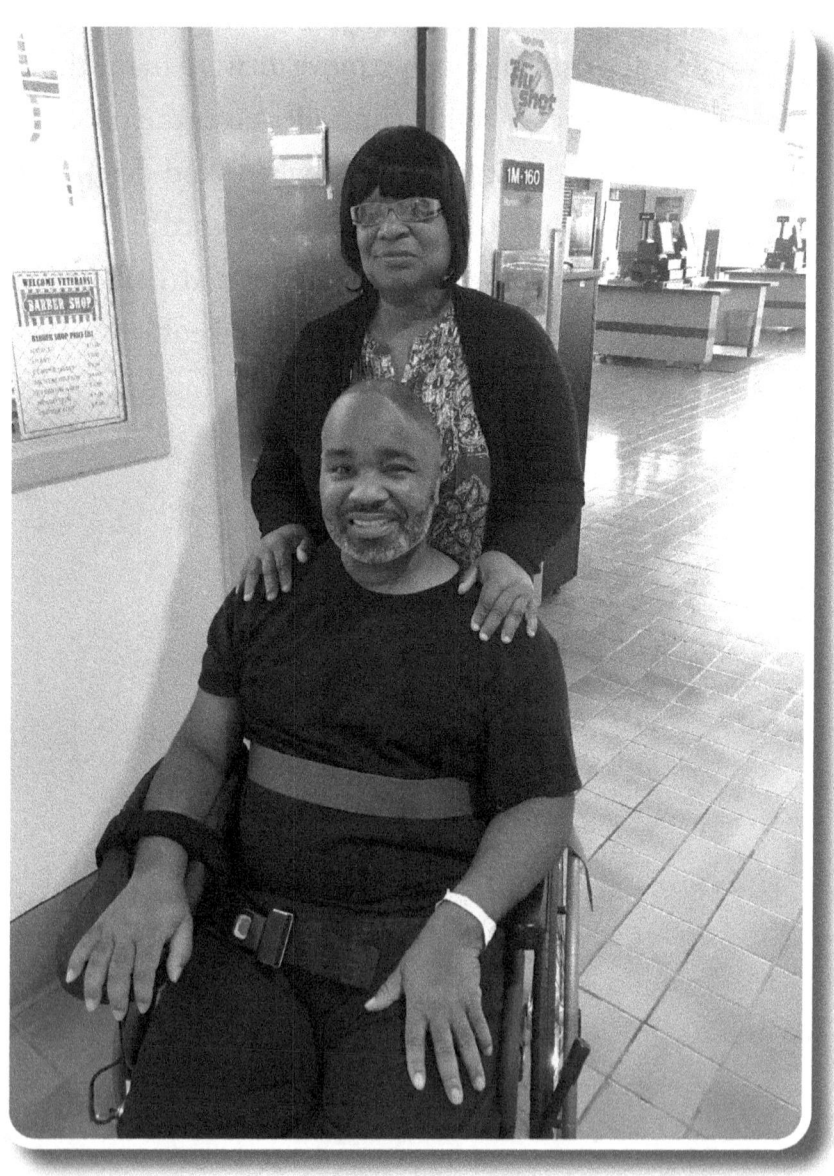

CHAPTER 8

Mourning the Loss of My Husband

IT TOOK ME AT least two years to realize that although my husband was still alive (as God had promised); his existence was markedly different after the stroke. The man I formerly loved and married was gone. The damage from the stroke caused significant physical limitations.

Samuel Andrew Stackhouse III, the one who would keep me in stitches laughing with his humor - yes him – was different. You see, I'm the super serious one (most of the time), the task driven one all the time. He could bring the laughter out of me more frequently than anyone. And I assuredly missed the way that he cared for me; like always knowing that my gas light was on E. While he realized during our dating season that I hated going to the gas station, it was also part of his love language. He would come home from work and retrieve my car keys to take my car to fill up the tank.

And the frequent times that I would receive roses and other flowers at home and at work (randomly at the various satellite locations) are too many to mention!

One of the things that he would do consistently was pray for and with me. His desire to do so was key to us growing close. Each time we would have one of our long phone conversations, he would always ask me if he could pray with me. He still prays for and with me, but it is hugely different with his speech limitations.

And oh, my goodness my husband could sing! That was another attractive feature. We would go to the park in White Marsh and sit in the car and he would serenade me with different songs. Yeah, by then I was falling in love with this guy for sure. He loved God and was a worshipper; super high marks for him, and us.

He loved God and was filled with the Word of God which he spoke frequently in different instances in my life without hesitation. Operating in his prophetic gift, he'd even spoken things into my life that manifested. I was convinced that he could be the man that I had been praying and waiting and waiting and praying for. He showed up in a short statured guy, which almost caused me to miss God and my guy. My conversation to God went like this, "you know I like tall men that I have to look up to." However, I did not allow that to deter me from the possibility that he could be my husband. Sometimes we miss God looking for Him to show up how we desire instead of allowing God to show up according to His plan for our lives.

But do not let the short stature fool you; he was tall on the inside, very sure and confident in himself. He stepped right to me telling me his whole life story in our first encounter. I mean he spelled out his entire life right there in the hair salon, in front of my dear friend and hair stylist without even taking a breath. I was like what in the world. Then he proceeded to ask for my number. I paused; normally I would have declined. In that moment I felt compelled to oblige him, somehow the moment felt quite different. I felt the heavens had opened right above where we stood. You see during his recanting of his life story, he disclosed that he had a non-profit focusing on mentoring inner-city boys in Baltimore City called Mentors for Life. He was not aware that I also had a non-profit - PressTab Ministries that had a mentoring component for young girls that I conducted at the Crispus Attucks Recreation Center years prior.

While working with the young ladies, little boys would always show up asking if they could come in and join us and I would explain that it was just for girls. While they expressed their dissatisfaction with my response, I would give them snacks to prevent them from lingering at the entrance of the door. Well one day, upon my departure, two of the little boys decided to walk me out of the building to retrieve additional snacks. As we were leaving, one asked what we were doing in the room with the young ladies every week. I explained that we participated in various activities that included having discussions about different topics that were important to the young ladies. One of the little boys exclaimed in a matter-of-fact tone and expression, "we like to talk too." And I responded, "Oh?"

I felt my anxiety level increasing because my assignment was helping girls based on my experience as a woman. I felt like I did not know enough about boys to assist them in any meaningful way. So, I gave them the last few snacks that were remaining because in that moment that was all I could offer them. As they received their sought-after snacks and I walked down the steps of the recreation center and to my car I whispered a prayer to God asking Him to send me a man (husband) that could work alongside me with the boys while I am working with the girls. In that moment, standing in the hair salon on that Tuesday evening May 13,

2014, assuredly, I felt like God had finally shown up and answered my prayers. Could it be? I was not sure, but it was worth the opportunity to see if God were about to answer a prayer. I gave him my business card and I wrote my cell number on the card. I was waiting on God to bless me with a husband, but I was not desperate, and most will tell you the look on my face really was a deterrent to potential suitors. That was not intentional, but I had been through a lot and did not want any more drama. Thus, by the time we met, I had not dated for a long time.

After Sam left the salon with my number, my friend and I looked at each other like what just happened. We went about the business of styling my hair – which is why I was there. As I was sitting under the hair dryer, I received a text message from an unknown number that read: "Can I give you a call?" I typed back, "Who is this?" The reply was "This is Sam." I typed, "Sure. Why not?" He called, said it was nice meeting me and asked if I had eaten. Then he asked if he could bring me something to eat for dinner. It was dinner time, and I was at the salon getting my hair done. I replied, "no thank you I'm good." He then laughed, "You are the first person to turn down something from me." Me, being me, countered with, "You need to change your circle of friends." He was a giver; another plus for him. I knew it because givers recognize givers. Based on his comment though, I also knew that he had a lot of takers surrounding him. At the end of the conversation, he asked me to text him when I arrived home. I did that and he immediately replied with "can I give you a call" which he did frequently early while we were dating instead of just calling. I responded yes and he called. Little did I know that we would be on the phone until four a.m. You have never met a man that could talk so much about so many things. He did most of the talking pausing occasionally for my response. After talking all night long for the first two weeks he would get off the phone at four and get dressed to be at work at the main post office by 5:30. I would go to sleep until it was time for me to get up for work. Before each call ended, without fail, he would ask, "Can I pray with you?" And I would assuredly respond, "Sure." so we prayed at every encounter. I prayed more because my original thought to God was either he is from you God, or the enemy sent him to trip me up.

We continued talking getting to know each other until he sent me a text one day saying he didn't want to be friends. When I read the text, I threw my phone down. What did he want? What did he mean? I didn't respond. He followed up with a phone call to explain himself. He wanted to date exclusively, which was not a problem for me, but during that time he had a friend who he was seeing. He ended that relationship, and we started dating exclusively. Sam was the perfect gentlemen. We both decided not to engage in sexual activity. He admitted that was the first time he had ever agreed to that, and it was the first for me too. I was excited finally to meet a man who loves God, and while not being perfect would fall in love with me and take loving care of me.

As I reflect, it highlights the things I miss about my husband. Simple things like him opening doors for me. The way he would check on me throughout the day to see if I needed anything. Showing up at my office with roses and lunch so often even my staff fell in love with him. He was a lover of people he was always excited about meeting someone new. He has never met a stranger. He was so sure of himself, kind, and a gentle soul. He wanted to care for anyone he encountered who had a need. He was a good provider and is even now, since his early decisions allowed him to be able to retire at an early age. He is a retired Army Veteran who also retired from the United States Postal Services. Sam also retired from Giant food corporation. When I met him, he was all set to retire then but felt uncertain about retiring when he wanted to take me as his wife, so he prolonged that big step. That's who he was a man's man, old school provider for his family. You don't find too many of them today, but God preserved one just for me and I was extremely excited about that.

He was a hardworking man with a desire to be a blessing and many took advantage of him and his kindness. And because I am a giver as well, I knew the frustration that accompanied that, so I became his shield against those who only wanted to use him. I'd come to learn more about his passion to mentor young black boys in Baltimore City. Quite a bit of my knowledge came during the numerous occasions that we would meet one of the young men, who had become adults. They would rave about how he cared for them in the absence of their own biological fathers, how he even provided shoes, clothes, and food when they had none. Just to hear them talk about him in this manner helped me to understand the jewel of a man that God was blessing me with. Sam was not a perfect man (that does not exist), but he was (and is) a good man and I felt because he loved God that we could make a life together. I believed that, with God, whatever was wrong with either of us God could and would fix and make it well. So, we prayed about it and decided to live "happily ever after" together not really knowing what that would mean.

We got married in Negril Jamaica. Yep, he granted my desire to have a destination wedding since he had been married and divorced prior. I don't think he cared how we got married. I'm sure he was more concerned that we were successful in our marriage over anything else. Sam was not pleased with himself about his failed marriage. In fact, his previous prayer was for God to restore that marriage. How God responded to his prayer was to send me into his life and I knew early on that I was the answer to his prayers; even though the manifestation was slightly different from the request. You see God knows what is best for us.

I digress, I was recalling the things I missed about the Sam I met. I missed those phone calls asking "how's my baby"; or his calling just to say I love you. I missed the text messages that he would send exclaiming how he has been happy since the day he met me. I also missed how he ensured that I was safe and secure. I later learned that was a part of his Army securing-the-boundaries training. One day, during our dating season, Sam came over to my house and upon his departure he went downstairs to the basement then he came back upstairs and left without saying why he did that. This happened while I was still praying about who sent him. I was wondering if he went downstairs to open or unlock a window so he could enter my house. You know people are crazy out here in these streets. I have watched enough Lifetime television network movies to know how this could play out, but he wasn't going to get me. I locked my front door, waited for him to pull off and then went to my basement to check the window which was the only way in and out. When I pulled the curtain back, I found the big wooden stick that I purchased from Home Depot and lodged at the top of the window so no one could lift the window from the outside, was still in place. I felt bad for thinking that he had removed it to gain access. While we dated and during the first two years of our marriage, whenever my husband would enter the house, he would make sure the basement was secure without failure.

Sam was my safe place. He was gentle and loving. When I found myself having to care for him after he suffered a massive stroke that part was easy to do. I knew he would have taken care of me if the tables were turned. Plus, the perfectionist in me would not rest unless I was certain everything concerning him was perfectly executed. And I cared for him in that manner. I still see some of the humor and jokester that he used to be but not in full measure. And he still ensures every night that I have secured the house and turned on the alarm system. He prays for me still, laying his hands on my feet and doing so while I slept. I miss him cooking for me. He could make a meal out of anything, and it would be good. I miss him being my chauffeur and driving me all around town. Oh, how I miss how he would talk my ears off, and I would finally ask, "Sam, what are you talking about?" That was my gentle way of letting him know that was enough talking for the day. I have promised God, in the aftermath of the stroke, that I would never do that again. God miraculously brought speaking back to my husband, after the doctors declared that he would never talk again, language expression nor comprehension. I made my own declaration for my husband - HE SHALL SPEAK AGAIN - and I meant that thing! And I still do, though we are years on this journey. I still declare and await this, full restoration of Samuel Andrew Stackhouse III and not even restored to what I formerly knew. I declare that he will be restored to whom God intended and created Sam to be. I pray and await yet for God's good purpose and pleasure to be fully realized through my husband's life and our lives joined. God is kind; and as I'm learning His heart, His desire, and His will for both Sam and I; I admit it's been disastrous and amazing. The disaster is the situation that led to me having to care for a husband after celebrating only two years of marriage. I'm glad we enjoyed that celebration in Jamaica because we did not know what we would face upon our return.

It is also important to know your why when it comes to marriage. We all get married for distinct reasons. But we must understand that marriage is ministry and a priority. If two don't agree on that, when a crisis hits, the errant reasons you got married will be shattered before your eyes. Then, what will you hold on to. Marriage ordained by God has a purpose and it is important to understand that purpose and your role in it. The main reason so many marriages are not able to survive crisis is because when the reasons that you got married are drastically changed, it becomes easy to walk away. You no longer hold dear the sanctity of what you vowed, to love through sickness and health, for richer and poorer. Although I miss the things that my husband was able to do for me, they were not my why I got married. I made a vow to him and to God; if God gives me the grace for this, I'm here forever. I'm here trusting that God has a plan for all of this.

I have seen the miraculous power of God when the doctors declared death or only a ten percent chance of living. As a believer in the Almighty God, I know that Sam and I will have life and that much more abundantly, including more of the miraculous power of the Living God.

I have grieved the loss of my husband in many ways; and as much as I grieved, I am anticipating and embracing the new life that we share, I have allowed myself to feel every stage of grief, but not to get stuck in either. I went through the disbelief of Sam's massive stroke. I tussled with being angry with God for allowing it to happen. I had waited and trusted God for a husband for years only to be faced with a spouse facing insurmountable recovery. I dealt with heartbreak. But God has and is healing me through the process. I have been able to accept where my husband and I are in our life currently. It is vastly different from what I had ever imagined but life is like that sometimes. And what I always say to others is that life is not about what happens to you but how you respond to what happens. This does not make things easy at all. I want to be pleasing to God and in my pursuit of Him I continue to find grace even for this assignment. Even in this God has been kind to Sam and me; and for this we continue to give Him praise. It is our desire for Him to get the glory out of our lives and whatever that costs us we surrender that to Him.

CHAPTER 9

The Weight of the Wait

AN EXCHANGE OF THE weight of the burden carried during the waiting period for the weight of God's glory – it's not an easy exchange – but it is a necessary one! It means while you are waiting for your miracle you must deal with the weight of the burden. I had to face the fact that until God moves and completes the miracle of healing my husband, I had to face the reality that he was not able to verbally express himself. The harsh reality that my husband could not talk, seemed surreal. However, I had to embrace it. It was hard for me to do that initially for many reasons. Communication is a major part of who we are as people. We communicate both verbally and non-verbally. It is also a major component of marriage; without it, many marriages struggle with some ending in divorce. Lack of communication is a major problem to have, whether it is due to medical reasons or a lack of skills.

I kept asking the questions how this could be and how do we survive this major challenge in our lives and still maintain our faith. How do we still believe that God is going to be true to His Word? I carried this burden every day from over three long years. I was constantly reminded that weight would press down upon me when my husband uttered the same phrases over and over. He simply was not able to express his feelings and thoughts in the normal way. How – I would ask myself - do we adjust to this new way of life and not become cynical because our reality? A reality that had not met up with the manifestation of our faith. Day in and day out I felt tortured or mocked by the enemy every time my husband tried to communicate. And every time I had to remind myself and the enemy that God will have His day in our lives. I have to remind myself that the fullness of time will come; and all will be well. Sometimes this encouragement of myself is easy because I just remember the miracle that God has already performed. However, If I am honest and transparent there are days when I am feeling alone because my husband's inability to talk has inadvertently affected my ability to speak. The truth is how can I communicate with a man that is not able to communicate in return. This has often caused me to keep my thoughts and feelings to myself. The global aphasia that has affected my husband has silenced me as well.

An unexpected and unwelcomed side effect for me, was the silence between and around us caused me to think about all my prior experiences that were designed to silence me. Those triggers made me want to shout out loud from the mountain top the goodness of the Lord to again encourage myself. Yet, on some days, I would shout out of the pain I felt in my heart that my husband and I are not able to dialogue – talking to each other was a big part of our love language. We were married for companionship and communication is a large part of that. What do you do when it has been eradicated? No words, no writing, and even cognitive abilities are challenged. The ebbs and flows between what do I have here and what is this; and thanking God for not allowing my mind to be overwhelmed from my disbelief. The reality of it all was heavy, the burden weighty, but the faith in more miracles manifesting had to outweigh it all.

What about the embarrassment and shame? Or the thoughts that your faith has failed you? Then there are the questions about whether you prayed hard enough? Did I not believe hard enough? Let's not even discuss all the questions around whether my husband believed enough for himself. We were not able to discuss anything. How could I know? You see these are all the things that can occur while you are waiting on God to do what you desire Him to do. In that, is one of the most frightening question. Is what I am desiring Him to do aligning with His will and plan for our lives? The enemy would like to use whatever he can to distract or confuse us so that we do not receive full manifestation of our prayers. The many questions can sometimes try to drive you crazy, but you manage to push through by the grace of God. You go through your stages of grief from anger to denial and bargaining to acceptance of where you are. Faith is not the denial of the facts that you are facing it is the currency that says I'm exchanging what I currently have before me for what God has said and makes possible in my life. Acceptance of the facts does not eradicate your miracle. We must live with the facts in my meantime season, but do not think for one moment that you should lose sight of the miraculous possibilities my faith will not fail me, my heart will not lose sight of God's word and I am constantly looking forward to a move of God in our lives that will change our situation. You must cling to that kind of faith too.

When you believe God for the impossible it may separate you from those who do not have the same level of faith and draw you closer to those who do. The Bible declares that each man has a measure of faith; that measure varies from person to person. This measure of faith also grows and develops with each experience that is designed to test and increase your faith.

You cannot get distracted if someone's faith does not measure up to yours. You must continue believing God until what you believe for manifests. Once you see manifestation of what you have believed for your faith is increased. God is faithful and He responds to faith as His Word declares.

Do not allow the wait to change your faith position. Just because you have a waiting period does not mean that God did not hear you or that He will not respond. We do not like to wait for anything let alone on God to bring to pass the things that He has promised us. Sometimes we allow that wait to cause anxiety, which can lead to doubt in God's promises.

Don't confuse the process with the promise. Sometimes in the waiting we can feel like what we have is the promise when what we are experiencing is the process of receiving the promise. During the waiting period there can be silence from God. We oftentimes interpret the silence and waiting as divine denial. It is important that we understand the difference between process and promise.

The heaviness of the wait, the time that we spend waiting and living without what we are waiting for can seem weighty. If you are sick and waiting for healing to occur in your body the symptoms and feelings underway can be a distraction. A delay feels like denial because it is accompanied with that resemblance of silence from God. But I guess God feels like He has already spoken, there is no need for Him to say anything further. But in my experience, it makes you wonder if you heard God right or did you hear what you wanted to hear. Nobody wants to believe that their situation is a dead one for sure. But my faith in God reminds me that God can bring life to things that are dead. Yet, we must remember in God's sovereignty dead things that are brought back to life must often live in Him in a new way. It is about discerning what your situation is and how God will respond as you release your faith. Faith don't make sense in the natural because it is the currency of the supernatural. You must tap in spiritually, press in to hear God even in the silence. What is God saying there? What is God doing behind the scenes and when will He unfold for His glory? Living in His glory costs us so much. The season after Sam's stroke was an emotional time but I pressed and continue to press in.

During the waiting period keep yourself focused on the finished work of God. Stand in the faith that it is already completed; you are just waiting for manifestation in the Earth realm. Seek God for what you are to do while you are waiting. Faith without works is dead. Do something to prepare for what you trust God for. Heaven forbid God responds, and you are not prepared for what you are praying for. Also make sure what you are trusting God for aligns with His word and His plan for your life. Prayers that do not align with the word of God or His Plan for your life are desires of your own agenda and will cause you to be frustrated. Make sure you are surrendered to God and trust that He has a plan for your life. Trust Him to work out every little detail as you walk out your faith journey. God is faithful and has proven that He can be trusted. He has already established Himself; His track record is perfect even when we must wait on Him.

Be cautious and keep yourself in faith by reading His Word and remaining in prayer. The Word of God declares that faith comes by hearing and hearing by the Word of God. Well, if that is the case and we know that His Word is true then the opposite can be true as well. If you meditate on doubts, fear, and anxiety, those things are magnified, and this will cancel out your faith. Both cannot exist together, neither occur at the same time. Choose to be intentional about feeding your faith and let that dominate your existence; it will erase all doubt and fear. In the end we must continue in faith until our change manifests. In the meantime, purpose is revealed, and God is glorified.

CHAPTER 10

Finality

GOD USES EVERYTHING THAT we face in life as an opportunity for growth and spiritual development. When we face situations that bring us to our knees, we need to fully understand that is where He wants us. As we mature in Him, we learn to seek Him, especially in those moments of fear and uncertainty. Remember that our faith in God is the key to manifestation and in most cases, we will not be able to make sense of it at all. We will always wonder how God will work things out and it is never according to our methods or timing. God is sovereign; and our trust in Him yields the peace we need and allows Him the space and time to do what He promises to do in our lives.

Every single time we have needed God, He has proven Himself to be faithful. He will continue to come through now and in the future; and as we look back over our lives that truth remains. God has placed us in the Earth with a purpose in mind and we ought to seek after that purpose; for surely a problem in the Earth is awaiting its solution through your purpose. We have to know that adversity will surely come, however, we are equipped to overcome and be victorious indeed!

Nothing is a surprise to God! He is all-knowing and ever present with wisdom and knowledge that supersedes all knowledge and wisdom in the Earth. So, when we seek Him for guidance and direction we are assuredly headed in the right direction and failure is far from us. And even when we face interruptions, we understand that it is at His allowance; in those times of uncertainty, we can find peace knowing that He has us covered. Having faith in God is being able to hope for something that there may be no evidence for, however as we believe God and He manifests Himself this increases our faith in Him even greater. Yes, our faith in God grows and develops, which allows us to see impossibilities become possible. And whatever God is calling us to do it is possible and He has given us the grace to complete every assignment in our lives regardless of the challenges that may exist. We must allow God to do the new thing in our lives without resistance or hesitation, knowing that we are in good hands with Him. We cannot allow fear of the unfamiliar or wanting to remain in our comfort zones to allow us to forfeit the next move of God. God desires to take us higher in Him and His plans for our lives are good even when we experience adverse conditions. We have to know that He will use those conditions to develop us into who He has created us to be. If the conditions are not perfect that does not necessarily mean that this is not God; perhaps God is redirecting you onto another path that aligns with His desire for your life. You must be willing to seek hard after Him. You will find God in the hard places in life and know that He is right there fighting with and for you ensuring that you have the victory as promised. With this, who hesitates to have faith in a God who proves Himself daily, allowing every situation that comes in your life to be the catalyst that establishes you on the path of destiny for your life. A life lived in purpose is our ultimate goal; anything short of that should not be acceptable. God awaits your full and effectual trust in Him.

ABOUT THE AUTHOR

DR. TONI ALLAYNE BOULWARE Stackhouse is the co-founder of New Life Ministries alongside her husband Elder Samuel Andrew Stackhouse III. Pastor Samuel A Stackhouse III is a retired Army veteran who loves people and serving others through prayer and giving. Dr Stackhouse is a Licensed Clinical Professional Counselor for the state of Maryland. Her passion for ministry is outreach and this passion extends to the marketplace where she has been serving those individuals experiencing homelessness in many different capacities for the last 20 years. During which time she has also provided extensive work in the mental health and substance abuse field. Dr. Stackhouse has a Doctor of education degree in Counseling Psychology from Argosy University, a Master's degree in human services with a concentration in counseling from Lincoln University, a bachelor's degree in organizational leadership from Nyack College, and an associates of arts degree in human services from The Community College of Baltimore County. Dr. Stackhouse is the founder of her own private counseling practice, Life Matters Wellness Center with a wholistic approach to mental health and wellness.

Dr. Stackhouse has great faith in God and demonstrates that faith in her obedience to God's Word. In Isaiah 43:19 God says, "Behold, I will do a new thing; now it shall spring forth; shall ye not know it? I will even make a way in the wilderness, and rivers in the dessert." In this season of her life, she is watching God manifest Himself in the new thing! Dr. Stackhouse describes herself as a woman who believes God and as the scriptures declares miracles, signs and wonders follow them that believe. The life that God is allowing her to live is transformation at its best, and she is trading nothing for her journey! She is a teacher, preacher, intercessor, mentor, therapist, coach, workshop presenter and author.

Dr. Stackhouse along with her husband Elder Samuel A. Stackhouse III have two adult children, Trenae' L. Watson and Son-son Arlen L. Watson and Marcus Stackhouse. They also have two grandsons AJ and Ayven. In their spare time they love traveling, shopping and entertaining family and friends.

www.ingramcontent.com/pod-product-compliance
Lightning Source LLC
Chambersburg PA
CBHW051946160426
43198CB00013B/2330